AF413142

UNVEIL
THE PRISTINE
GLORY WITHIN

Ancient Indian Wisdom Simplified

Modern Perspective of Bhaja Govindam
The Seven Mighty Hermetic Principles Revisited
Inner Exploration to Unravel the Ultimate Truth

VOL. 2

Dr. K.R.S. NAIR

Amazon # 1 bestselling author

ALSO BY THE AUTHOR

- ❖ **BOUNDLESS POWER OF MINDFUL LIVING**
  Pamper Your Inner Self, Stay Connected to Spirit and Soar Higher, Grow Inside-Out, and Reap *the Best of Life.*

- ❖ **INCREDIBLE WORD POWER: A UNIQUE HUMAN ENDOWMENT**
  Know Three Strengths and Four Keys, How to Prudently Script One's Destiny, and Be a Wholesome Winner for Life

- ❖ **THE ART AND SCIENCE OF PRAYER: Why Our Prayers Are Seldom Answered?**
  Religion, Spirituality, and Science on the Highway To God

- ❖ **What Self-Help Books Won't (& Can't)Tell You**
  Role of Indomitable Samskara, Vasana, and Karma in Self-Development; Pathfinding to Veritable Happiness & Success

FROM THE PRAISE FOR 'ANCIENT INDIAN WISDOM SIMPLIFIED: UNBURDEN YOURSELF (Vol.1)'

........Within the pages of this enlightening masterpiece, Dr. K.R.S.Nair ...has exhibited a remarkable prowess, skillfully crafting an exceptionally captivating commentary for every verse in a manner that is both unique and erudite......What distinguishes this opus from others in its genre is Dr. Nair's adept interweaving of explicit anecdotes and thought-provoking parables throughout the treatise.

.....In the vast realm of spiritual literature, this book emerges as a beacon, illuminating the path for those earnestly engaged in the pursuit of spiritual knowledge....

(Dr. K.V.Sahasranam, Cardiologist)

.....The book revolves around the principles of karma, wisdom, desire, resilience, reciprocity, self-realization, personal responsibility and what not......The pursuit of desires only leads to more craving, perpetuating a cycle of discontent........

(K. Jayaram)

........Dr. Nair's eloquence transforms complex concepts into practical guides, making 'Unburden Yourself' not just a book but a roadmap to self-discovery....... it's an invitation to shed life's burdens and embrace the essence of Vedanta.

(Ratan K. Sharma)

......the entire book is..... more than a 'well of wisdom'. .....A wonderful book that one must read.

(Firoz Kujur)

....Amazing book. Inspirational and motivational with spirituality. There are excellent stories to relate to different subjects and great research on various aspects of life.

(Reena Gupta)

........This book, presented in the form of a conversation between the Guru and the students, is a lucid version to understand the nitty-gritty of Vedanta. ......The learning points at the end of every chapter are a recollection of all the wisdom.

(NDSV Nageswara Rao, G. M., SBI)

Dedicated at the lotus feet of
my Guru
Navajyothisree Karunakaraguru
of Santhigiri Ashram, Kerala, India

TABLE OF CONTENTS

Dr. K.R.S. Nair

Dr. K R S Nair has had ***outstanding academic achievements in diverse fields*** like Animal Husbandry, Banking & Commerce, Business Administration, and Training & Development. During his academic career, he won the Kerala State Merit Scholarship, Merit Scholarship from the Indian Council of Agricultural Research, His Highness the Maharaja'a Scholarship from Calicut University, and the Kerala Agricultural University Merit Scholarship.

An accredited behavioral science specialist and a corporate trainer for over 25 years, he was the best trainer of SBI, the biggest bank in the country. He is ***a winner of 12 national and international awards***, including the Commonwealth Bureau of Animal Health Prize (England), awards from Indian Council of Agricultural Research, Indian Society for Training and Development, State Bank of India, Interfaith Leadership Award from the World Yoga Community INC (New York), etc.

Dr. Nair has ***authored 14 non-fiction books*** in English, of which six have been Amazon's International No. 1 bestsellers several times, while most of the others were national bestsellers. He has also penned 10 books for the SBI Training System, a collection of short stories, about 100 papers including internationally acclaimed research papers on poultry science, about 160 blog posts, and articles on other general and management themes published in reputed magazines like the 'Indian Management,' SBI Monthly Review, Journal of Cochin Stock Exchange, etc. He also contributed articles to the compiled editions published by Kerala Agricultural University, Pentagon Press, Delhi, and Bharatiya Kala Prashasan, Delhi.

He is a life member of Indian Institute of Banking and Finance, and a member of the Bestseller Club of 'Author Freedom Hub', a collective of Indie authors.

For six years, Dr. Nair was the Chief Editor of 'Rural Banker,' an all India journal of the State Bank Institute of Rural Development, one of the Apex Training Institutes (ATI) of SBI in Hyderabad.

His other cerebral pursuits include papers presented in international seminars and colloquiums, radio talks, and public speaking on spiritual and management topics.

The positions held during his career include assignments like Veterinary Surgeon, Poultry officer, Asst. Professor at Kerala Agricultural University, and different managerial positions in the SBI. Retired as Asst. General Manager from the Bank. Presently, he serves as Senior General Manager (HR) at Santhigiri Ashram,

Thiruvananthapuram, a spiritual organization of international repute.

Dr. Nair conceived and launched a novel project for rural development christened 'Farmers' Corner' in a rural branch of SBI, which earned wide acclaim as the 'social laboratory of SBI'. The project was adopted by the Bank and rolled out across its rural and semi-urban branches in the country.

His biographical note and photograph got published in five 'Who's Who' Books released by three publishers in Delhi and also in different titles of American Biographical Institute, U.S.A.

He lives in Thiruvananthapuram, Kerala.

Mobile: + 91 9446810090

Email: keyares51@gmail.com

<h1 style="text-align:center"><u>PREFACE</u></h1>

Bhaja Govindam is an insightful work of Vedanta, presented in a simple and rhythmic style. It comprises 31 verses. The opening stanza is a chorus and chanted at the end of every other verse.

Hailed both as a *stotra* (devotional song) and a *prakarana* (introductory text on spiritual studies), it deals with two-fold motivations of human life – *kanchana* (acquisition of wealth) and *kamini* (enjoyment of lust and wealth); Sankaracharya points out the futility of pursuing both. The great saint is urging us to get over our obsession with the trivialities of life and to begin our search for the ultimate Reality, which is the real purpose of life.

At the outset, let's understand that ***the theme of this book is not for the Hindus only. It holds a universal appeal, as it addresses everyone***. The word 'Govindam' stands for the Atman, which is the Truth behind the ever-changing flux of things that constitutes the universe of our experience. Govinda is the Brahman of the Upanishads and is the highest

Reality. So, 'Bhaja Govindam' means seek your identity with the creator, the Brahman, the Supreme.

The text under review is an entry point into Vedanta, which also throws light on many teachings of the scriptures. In a highly simplified form, it distils the teachings of the fundamental texts of Vedanta, Bhagavad Gita, etc. The present edition is the Volume II under the series titled 'Ancient Indian Wisdom Simplified'. **Attempted here is a thorough study and understanding of the expositions on one of the most popular *stotras* composed by Sankara, which can remove all the delusions of the materialistic world.**

As C. Rajagopalachari said, 'When intelligence matures and lodges securely in the heart, it becomes wisdom. When that wisdom is integrated with life and issues out in action, it becomes devotion. The knowledge that has become mature is devotion. If it does not transform into devotion, such knowledge is useless tinsel.'

1

A RECAP OF 'UNBURDEN YOURSELF'

Volume 1 of the book in this series titled 'Ancient Indian Wisdom Simplified' UNBURDEN YOURSELF' covered the opening ten chapters of 'Bhaja Govindam' by Adi Sankara. Before taking up the subsequent chapters of the text by the Acharya for a commentary in the modern context, it would be befitting to review the contents of the previous Volume, for two reasons. First, as the discussion on the poem is continued in this Volume, a recap would facilitate the reader to refresh and connect better with the areas already covered in the previous volume. Secondly, a new reader who takes up this volume without studying the first one would find this relook helpful to gain an insight into its contents and could be motivated to access it for a detailed study.

The significance of Bhaja Govindam is that it is an entry point into Vedanta, which also throws light on many teachings of the Indian scriptures in a highly simplified form. It presents a distilled version of the fundamental texts of Vedanta, Bhagavad Gita, etc. in such a manner that one who is not familiar with the scriptures also can gain some insight into them, understand the import of the great poem, and reinvent his life. The objective of the present three-volume series is to help discerning readers do a self-audit of the conduct of their lives and escape from the delusions of the materialistic world by making appropriate changes so that they could realize the ultimate purpose of human life.

The style of narration in the book

The commentary is patterned as a classroom discussion on spiritual intelligence by a trainer and his trainees in an interactive style. Apart from better readability, the method facilitates clearing the possible doubts and ambiguities that could arise in the minds of the readers as they go on reading the book. This is sought to be achieved in such a manner that such possible doubts and blind spots are addressed then and there by way of questions from the trainees in the classroom and the answers from the trainer.

The opening verse of the poem may appear to belittle acquiring worldly knowledge, as a student in the class doubted in the book. The import of any statement depends on the context in which it arises. Content taken out of context renders it irrational, as is often arraigned by people, especially political leaders and others. 'Bhaja Govindam' was composed by Sankaracharya when he was walking through the streets of Varanasi, along with his disciples, and found an old man struggling to learn Sanskrit grammar. The Acharya went to him and said, "At this ripe old age, don't be foolish to waste your time to learn basic grammar."

"Lift the heart to Govinda, O foolish man!

When thou are at the death's door,

the rules of grammar that you're trying to master

will not come to your rescue!"

Just ponder on it: The science you have learned, the books you have studied and mastered, and the skills you've acquired – will any of these stand by you when the death knocks at your door? Could anybody in the world argue with the god of death when he went to them at the appointed time and delayed their leaving even by a minute, on the strength of the knowledge they acquired? Book learning without devotion to God will be of no avail in the presence of death. The Acharya warns against wasting all life in mere book learning, neglecting love and devotion to God.

Why do people go after material pursuits, despite seeing all around in life that knowledge, wealth, power, relationships, etc. will be of no avail in the end? The answer lies in *the karmagati* of people. Scriptures proclaim that creation (*ulpatti)* will happen as per the karmagati of the *jiva.* The first two chapters discuss the three components of one's karmagati, viz., the karma accumulated by a person over the lifetimes, their ancestors' karmagati, and the influence of the deities and other spirits worshipped by a person and their ancestors over lifetimes. Karma is governed by the law of cause and effect; it never gets extinguished by itself. Nor is it limited by time or space.

The third chapter is on knowledge and wisdom. Knowledge comes from the outside, whereas wisdom crops up from the inside. However, wisdom cannot be acquired and applied without knowledge. As C. Rajagopalachari said, "When wisdom is integrated with life and issues out in action, it becomes devotion. The knowledge that has become mature is devotion. If it does not transform into devotion, such knowledge is useless tinsel."

If the first verse exhorts to detest craving for knowledge, the second one cautions against the insatiable longing to amass wealth. It further asks people to be content with the fruits of their own labor to achieve lasting peace and happiness. Proceeding further, the Acharya talks about another common intractable inclination of people to get caught in the vortex of lust. Sankara says, "Excited by woman's beauty, her bosom, and the region of the navel, do not allow yourself to be lost; they are only forms of mere flesh." Discrimination is the only way to exorcise this 'evil spirit'. As Swami Vivekananda said, "... These desires of the body bring only momentary satisfaction and endless suffering."

In the fourth stanza, the sage compares the vulnerability of human life with a water drop resting on a lotus petal. Strong turbulence in its substratum, which may occur at any time, will throw the water drop, majestically dancing on the lotus petal, back to the surrounding water body, and extinguish its independent existence. Similarly, a person's pride, power, majesty, and the existence itself could get wiped out within no time.

The significance of the lotus in spirituality is explained in detail in the chapter. The lessons the life of Lotus offers to humans are manifold. It shows how humans ought to live in the world – to work relentlessly, without getting attached to the results and the surroundings. If you are persevering and resilient, notwithstanding the adverse circumstances, you can survive, be prosperous, and be victorious.

So long as you are wealthy and powerful, your family will love and hover around you. But once you lose your wealth and start getting old, your friends and relatives don't care for you, nor bother to ask you how you are doing. So, what did they love earlier – you, the person, or your money and power? The message the fifth verse of Bhaja Govindam conveys is that the world revolves around quid pro quo. "Give me something, and I will give you something in return." We have two aspects of ourselves: most of us are so locked up at the function level of our lives that we have lost touch with the being level of ourselves. As a result, we become hypocrites.

The uniqueness of Indian spirituality is that it evolved from the first-hand experience of our Rishis of yore, who deduced the Truth of Existence through spiritual visions (*darshan*) from their relentless pursuit of realizing the Ultimate. The Rishis' revelations were experiential, not experimental. They understood and declared that all material accomplishments, including garnering knowledge, amassing wealth, seeking sensual pleasures, and the like are not only transitory but also of little use in realizing the ultimate purpose of life.

Sankara further says, "People at your home will show concern for your welfare so long as there is breath in your body. Once the life force departs the body, even your wife will be scared of that body." Attachments and nourishments of the body continue until the breath remains in it. The moment the life force leaves the body, it turns inert and inanimate and acquires a common name that it shares with all dead bodies – a corpse. The human body is like a cloth worn by the indwelling *jiva*. It is comparable to a guest house wherein in the soul stays for a pre-determined period and vacates thereafter.

In the seventh verse, Acharya talks about human nature: 'During childhood, everyone is fond of playing; once he becomes a youth, he is attracted to the opposite sex; in the old age, one is mired in anxieties and worries....No one gets attached at any time to Supreme Brahman.' Such is the pull of the veil of 'Maya'. Every stage of life is transitory. Due to the power of 'Maya,' people revel in them as if they are permanent. To think that 'this too shall pass' is a great life mantra, an equalizer in life that should be remembered by people, at all times. Lasting peace and happiness can be achieved only through realizing the Self.

The eighth stanza asks: "Who is your wife? Who is your son? Very strange indeed is this 'samsara' (family bond). Whom do you belong to? Who are you? From where have you come? Oh, brother! Reflect on the truth of it all." In the verse, Sri Sankara suggests not to confuse the body, which came from the earth and is perishable, with the imperishable soul, and not to be a victim of attachment. Who you are can be found out by redirecting your attention to the inner Self, and concentrating on it until it gets realized.

The baggage of karmic imprints or inherent *vasanas* carried by a *jiva* as it incarnates in a human body influences and directs a person's behavior. How can one get extricated from this influence? Sankara shows the way out in the next verse. He says, "Through the company of the wise (*satsanga*), there arises non-attachment (*nis'sangatvam*). Through non-attachment, there arises freedom from delusion (*nirmohatvam*). When that happens, there you behold the unchangeable reality (*nischalatatvam*). Once the unchangeable reality is experienced, there comes liberation or freedom *(Jeevan Mukti)*. This can be termed the 'ladder of deliverance.'

The aforesaid is the path to overcome one's fate or karma, and is the most promising philosophy as it underscores that the locus of control of your life is well within you; you are the architect of your life. How this can be achieved in life is explained with further explanations and answers to the questions raised by the trainees in the classroom. The common misconceptions about *jeevan mukti* as a state to be realized after death are also removed with the support of expositions from *Vivekachoodamani,* another classic of Sankaracharya.

In contrast to the ascending ladder of deliverance posited by Adi Sankara, the Bhagavad Gita talks about the descending ladder of destruction (Chapter 2.62 & 2.63). The various steps thereof are object- attachment- desire - anger- delusion- loss of discriminative power and memory- loss of conscience- the ultimate fall.

Nothing happens in the world without a cause. When youth is gone, of what use is lust? Where is the lake when the water has dried up? Where is one's retinue when the wealth is gone? Similarly, when Truth is realized, where is *samsara?* (the worldly bond). Sorrow and suffering haunt you only so long as the mind is deluded. When the delusion is gone, the sorrows and suffering disappear like mist before the sun. Sri Sankara is talking in the tenth sloka of Bhaja Govindam about this phenomenon of human life.

The essence of this verse is that the sorrows of life will cease to exist upon the realization of the knowledge of the Self. The cause of all human suffering is ignorance of the true Self. If we can remove the cause, the effect will be gone, and we will no longer be the victims of *samsara*.

The contents of *Ancient Indian Wisdom Simplified: UNBURDEN YOURSELF Volume 1* ends with the above verse.

2

Why one should visit the cemetery often?

Sandeep: "Sir, what are the common characteristics of wealthy people?"

Trainer: "They are successful in life. They have more friends and robust relationships. In general, they are prideful because they wield power, position, name, and fame."

Malathi: "So, can we conclude that they are happy and have a fulfilling life?"

Anandavardhan: "Far from so. Wealth is not the criterion to measure happiness or fulfillment in life.

For that matter, even success is not a yardstick by which you can gauge one's life. Because triumph is made more visible than failure, people long for it and systematically overestimate their probability to succeeding. They are the staple of self-help books available in the market. Even if your success stems from pure coincidence or sheer luck, you will discover similarities with other successful people and conclude that these are success factors. And what happens to the credulous people who ape these 'success factors' to essay their success? As Rolf Dobelli put in 'The Art of Thinking Clearly', they end up in the graveyard of failed individuals and doomed companies. If you visit their graveyards, you will realize that the tenants of these burial grounds shared many of the same traits that characterized the successful people. Not only that, most of the so-called successful people also end up in the graveyards of failed people, as time robs them of their riches and wealth.

As Dobelli says, "The burial ground houses 10,000 times more musicians than the stage does, but no journalist is interested in failures —except the fallen superstars (read the story of Naresh Goyal, below). It makes the cemetery invisible to the outsiders." And therein lies the importance of visiting these places often so that you will not be another victim of 'Survivorship Bias."

Lal: "What is 'Survivorship Bias'?"

Trainer: "The tendency of ambitious people who read the success stories of others to systematically overestimate their chances of success is known as Survivorship Bias. It happens mainly because the media always projects the success stories of triumphant people. They methodically gloss over the stories of failures, which far outnumber the winning tales. It is in the backdrop of this reality that one has to reflect on the 11th verse of Bhaja Govindam, which states:

"Ma kuru/dhanajanayauvangarvam

Harati/nimeshatkalah/sarvam

Mayamayamidhamakhilam/hitva

Brahmapadam/tvam/pravisha/vidhitva."

"Do not take pride in wealth, friends, and youthfulness. Time snatches away all these in the blink of an eye. Free yourself from the illusion of the world of 'Maya', and discerning it, enter into the state of Brahman. So, *bhaja Govindam, muda mate.*"

Here, the word *dhana* also encompasses power, position, name, fame, etc. Do not also have pride in that there are people to follow you, to do your bidding, and to take commands from you. All these can disappear within no time. May you realize that all this creation is a product of 'Maya' and therefore seek what is unchanging and eternal. For which, sing the glory of 'Govinda' always.

Naresh Goyal, the fallen doyen of the Indian aviation sector

Naresh Goyal was the founder and Chairman of the once-famous Jet Airways. He systematically rose in the ladder of growth and bagged 16 prestigious awards from 2003 to 2012. However, luck was not in his favor for long. In 2019, he and his wife Anita Goyal stepped down from the Board of Jet Airways amid a financial crisis that engulfed the aviation major, and two-thirds of its fleet got grounded. On a complaint from the financier, Canara Bank, Goyal got arrested by the Enforcement Directorate in Sept. 2023. The man looks so broken and helpless in jail; he tells the Court that he lost all his hopes and prefers to die in jail.

The world has seen both his heydays and the subsequent pathetic state now. There's a big lesson to learn here. Never be proud of your achievements and success in life. Whatever one has accomplished will all get lost one day, for sure. Do not get entangled with the cycle of time.

Success re-defined

While writing this story, this author happened to listen to a monk explaining the terms growth, progress, and success. He said there is a big difference between these three terms. When you increase the turnover of your company from 5000 lakhs to 100,000 lakhs to 500,000 lakhs, it is called growth; it is not a success. Increasing your materialistic possessions in all ways is growth. That growth, if and when supported by ethics, which means discipline, honesty, and norms, is called progress. And that progress plus humanity, morality, and spirituality is what should be called success. Naresh Goyal in the above story had achieved growth, but not progress or success because he lacked discipline, ethics, morality, and spirituality in great measure.

A Chinese story on attaining Enlightenment

One day, a man from a village went to the ashram of a renowned Guru and requested the master to accept him as a disciple. The guru asked him a few questions and decided to take him in. Finding that he had little education, the guru assigned him to the ashram kitchen, where his duty was to clean the rice to be cooked for the 500-strong inmates and the visiting devotees.

The man got up every day early in the morning and started his work; he was totally on the job till late night. He had little time to go to the daily sermons, attend the prayers, read the scriptures, or listen to the talks delivered by the pundits. Likewise, 20 long years passed, and this man was there doing nothing but cleaning rice in the kitchen! He lost track of the days, dates, and everything else. He could seldom recollect his name as nobody used to hail him by the name.

One day the master declared to his disciples that the time had come for him to depart his body. He wanted to choose a successor for him and gave them a test for that purpose. "Anyone who thinks he has succeeded in self-remembering may write on the wall of my hut some insight that shows that he has seen the Truth."

A senior disciple, considered by all as the greatest scholar in the whole group tried. But he was aware that what he wrote on the wall was not his insight but something from the scriptures. In the morning, the master saw the writing and asked the servant to erase it immediately. He said, "Find out the idiot who spoiled my wall." The 'great scholar' has not even put his signature below what he wrote for fear of being caught.

Almost a dozen of the scholars tried to give expression to their insight, but none of them dared to sign his name. A visibly annoyed guru said, "None of you has attained the point of self-remembering. You have all been feeding your ego in the name of self. All my preaching so far has come to naught. Now, I will find a deserving successor for me myself."

At midnight, the guru went to the unlettered villager who joined the ashram kitchen two decades ago. For 20 years, the master had not seen him. He could not remember his face or name either. He went where the man was sleeping and woke him up. The latter asked, "Who are you?" As he had never met the master after his initial contact for a few minutes on the day he joined the ashram long back, the man couldn't recognize the guru's voice, and he continued, "What made you disturb my sleep at this odd hour?"

The master replied, "I am your master here. You have forgotten me. Do you remember your name at least?"

The man jumped up, apologized for not recognizing the guru, and said: "No. It's difficult for me to recollect my name. The karma you have assigned me is such that my name has no relevance here, nor any fame or scholarship is needed to accomplish it. It is so simple and engaging that I have forgotten everything else, including my name and other details. But I am indeed grateful to you guruji." He touched the feet of the master and said, "Please do not change my job. I have forgotten everything else, but I have also achieved everything."

He continued, "I now know a peace that I have never experienced in the past, a silence that no words can express. I have known such moments of ecstasy that even if I die this moment, I will never feel that this life has not been fair to me. Just do not change my job, I implore. Has anybody complained about my work or behavior, master?"

The master replied, "No. Nobody has complained about you, but your job has to be changed because I am choosing you as my successor."

The man was startled and said: "But master, you know that I'm only a rice-cleaner at this ashram and don't know anything about being a guru or a disciple. I know nothing but to clean rice. Please forgive me. I don't want to be your successor because I cannot handle such a big job; I am a small person with little knowledge and experience."

Master, determined as he was, said, "You have achieved what others have been trying to achieve and failed. You have achieved because you were doing your karma without any desire for its fruits. In simply doing your small work, there was no need for thinking, scope for emotions, need for anger or fighting, comparison, or ambition – your ego died a natural death. And with your ego, died your name. You were not born with a name. The ego is given a name, which is the beginning of the ego. With the death of your ego, you even forgot your own master, because it was your ego that brought you to me. Up to that moment, you were on a spiritually ambitious journey.

You are perfectly the right person to take the mantle of the spiritual head; so take my spiritual attire, which has traditionally been given by the master to the worthy successor. But a word of caution to you: take them and escape from this place as far away as you can, because your life will be in danger. All these 500 egoists will do away with you. You are so simple and innocent that if they ask for this spiritual attire, you will readily part with it.

You just take them and go as far away as you can into the mountains. Soon, people will start coming to you, just as bees start finding their way towards the flowers that bloom. You have blossomed. You need not bother about the disciples; you rest assured silently in a remote place. People will come to you. You can teach them whatever you have been doing."

"But", the unconvinced man said, "I have not received any teaching, and I do not know what I can impart to others."

The master said reassuringly, "Just teach them to do small things unassumingly, without any pride or ego, silently, peacefully, without any ambition, without any motivation to gain something in this world or the other world. Tell them that, by that way, they can become innocent like a child, and that innocence is the real religiousness and the gateway to get enlightenment."

(Courtesy: Sai Balasanskaar)

Essence:

One must treasure each moment of life and not while it away. Alertness and mindfulness should always be there; it will keep you focused on the ultimate truth. One must not be proud or become deeply engrossed in and attached to material possessions like wealth, relationships, power, or beauty. These are all but transient. The whole world is pervaded by illusion. To entangle oneself with the temporary instead of seeking the permanent is the greatest folly in life. Abasement of the ego is supremely important to attain enlightenment.

Major Takeaways from the Chapter

- ❖ *All material possessions, including relationships, are transient and could be snatched away by time in the blink of an eye.*

- ❖ *People often mistake growth for progress or success. Growth + ethics = progress. Real and lasting success is progress tempered with humanity, morality, and spirituality.*

- ❖ *Doing one's karma without any desire for its fruits and with utmost devotion and dedication, in a spirit of surrender, and without ego and pride will help one realize the Ultimate Truth.*

3

SELF-IDENTITY BUILT ON OTHERS' VIEWS

"Dinayaminyau /sayam/ pratah

Sisiravasantau/ punarayatah

Kalah/ kridati /gacchatyayuh

Tadapi/ na /munchatyasavayuh"

(BG 12)

"Day and night, dawn and dusk,

Winter and spring, come and go;

With the play of time, life ebbs away

And yet, one leaves not the gust of desires!"

Trainer: "Day and night come and go; so also do seasons. Man, who has the faculty of discernment and reflection, nevertheless fails to notice the impermanence of everything in Nature, and goes on clinging to desires. He does not let go of his desires, whatever the circumstances. Desires are one of the four fundamental motivations in human life, according to Bhaktivinoda Thakura, a Hindu philosopher. All material pursuits stem from one's desires. Why do people go after wealth, success, and pleasures? They are all aimed at personal gratification through fulfillment of desires."

Suhra: "What are the other three motivations of life, Sir?"

Anandavardhan: "*Fear, duty, and love.* People are *afraid* of poverty, sickness, old age, death, and the like, and want to avoid them, if possible. Similarly, *duty* is performed as part of one's show of gratitude, responsibility, etc. *Love* emanates from the care for others and the urge to help them. Everything that we do in life can be attributed to one of these four motivations, says the philosopher.

The Buddha said that pain or suffering arises through desire or craving, and to avoid it, we need to cut the bonds of desire. All cravings are the mind seeking salvation or fulfillment in external things.

Over to a story:

A man got chased by a tiger in the forest. While running to escape, he fell into a well and got stuck on a branch midway in his fall. He understood that if he slipped by a fraction of an inch, he would plunge into the watery grave below, where water snakes were swimming around. The tiger that followed him peered threateningly at him from the top of the well.

Suddenly, the man was stung by bees. He noticed that some rats were busy gnawing at the creeper, which prevented him from falling. And then he was also alarmed at finding that a bear came and started clawing into a honeycomb on the tree overhanging the well. Amidst this perilous state, with a threat to life lurking all around, a drop of honey drips on his face from the honeycomb above. The man, forgetting all the perils that he was in, stuck out his tongue and started to lick the drop of honey on his face!

This story exemplifies the craving for pleasure we're seeking in worldly life. The well in the story symbolizes one's family life. The rats represent TIME. And the honey dribbling amidst all the lurking dangers represents the momentary pleasures of sensual life. It shows how worldly pleasures lure and haunt us. They give us a pinch of pleasure accompanied by a pound of pain, and the latter we blissfully ignore. This is what Sankaracharya calls 'Maya'.

Sandeep: "But, what is wrong with having desires, Sir? As you said, they are the primary motivation to achieve success and happiness."

Trainer: "But what sort of happiness do you derive from turning successful? How long does it last? Jim Carrey, the famous Canadian-American actor once said, "I think everybody should get rich and famous and do everything they ever dreamed of, so they can see that it's not the answer." Chasing happiness through success is an illusion, and one will be left waiting for it forever."

Supriya: "Why is it so?"

Trainer: "Simple. When we consider that our accomplishments and successes will bring us lasting happiness, we are living in a fool's paradise (*Maya*) because lasting *happiness is internal* and does not come from material gratification, which is *external*.

Malathi: "Please explain it, Sir"

Trainer: "Just visualize this situation: You are forced to live in an uninhabited island, all alone. Will you have an urge to achieve and accomplish things; a sustainable urge? Our self-identity and self-esteem are built upon the edifice of others' opinions and assessments about ourselves. If they are not there, if no objects are there to draw our experience to make a self-assessment, we'll have little motivation to achieve and succeed.

Whenever we refer to objects to define our identity, we are operating out of, as Deepak Chopra termed it, 'object-referral' mode. Object-referred individuals evaluate, understand, and try to know themselves through the eyes of others. Their thinking and responses both are conditioned – conditioned by the assessment of the others. They are living under the hypnosis of social conditioning.

The craving to acquire knowledge, amass wealth and material possessions, and build relationships are all aimed at boosting our self-image and social status. As long as we identify ourselves with objects, we will never know our real essence because, by their very nature, objects change and accordingly, our self-image also. In other words, object referral is the primary cause of unhappiness in life. To elucidate the point, let's take up a story:

There was a man who had only two things that he valued the most in life. One was his son, and the other was a little pony. His whole sense of reality revolved around these two objects. One day, it so happened that his pony disappeared. The man, who suddenly lost half of his prime possessions, was devastated. He plunged into deep sorrow. Days passed by, and one day, his pony came back, and to the great excitement of its owner, it was accompanied by a beautiful white stallion. The man was in the heights of ecstasy now. See how things condition the lives of people.

The next day, his son hopped onto the stallion to ride it, but the untrained animal threw him away. The youngster broke his leg and was bedridden. Again, from the heights of ecstasy, the father was in the depths of despair. One day, the government's army came looking to recruit all the young men for an imminent war. They drafted every young man in the village except our man's son, who had a broken leg. Once again, he was delighted as his only son was spared by the government.

Human life is nothing but this oscillation between happiness and sorrow, which alternates like the day and night or summer and winter."

Malathi: "If object-referral is our seeking self-identity from out of objects, and is undesirable because it is unstable, what is its opposite state called?"

Anandavardhan: "The opposite is *self-referral*. In self-referral, we identify with our inner self, which is the unchanging essence of our soul. It is a state where we are not conditioned by our situation, circumstance, or environment. Self-referral leads to the internal state of joy and is different from happiness for a reason, which is transient. When you experience inner joy, you are happy for no reason. We all have had this experience of being joyful for no reason, albeit momentarily. The only thing is that we have not recognized that these are the moments when we are in touch with our inner Being.

As Eckhart Tolle says in *The Power of Now*, "Being is the eternal, ever-present One Life beyond the myriad forms of life that are subject to birth and death. However, Being is not only beyond but also deep within every form as its innermost invisible and indestructible essence. This means that it is accessible to you now as your own deepest self, your true nature. But don't seek to grasp it with your mind. Don't try to understand it. You can know it only when the mind is still, when you are present, fully and intensely in the Now...... To regain awareness of Being and to abide in that state of 'feeling- realization' is enlightenment."

According to Tolle, the greatest obstacle to experiencing your inner reality, your very essence, is identification with your mind, which causes thought to become compulsive. This incessant mental noise (of thinking) prevents you from finding that realm of inner stillness that is inseparable from Being. The mind is absent during moments of our inner joy when we are in touch with our inner self. As a result, we are not trying to understand the realm of inner stillness we're in.

If you look at the *sloka* no 11 that we discussed, we can see that apart from its literal meaning of alternating day and night, and the seasons, it can be understood figuratively as well. It's the recurring nature of happiness and sorrow, the ups and downs, and the extremes we encounter in daily life. Every time we experience happiness, we must realize that sorrow is just around the corner, awaiting its turn to jump on us. And this cycle continues unceasingly – as long as we're mired in the cycle of birth and death. That's the law of nature.

In the next session, we'll take up the 'Seven Mighty Principles' that throw more light on these aspects of the immutable laws of nature."

MAJOR TAKEAWAYS

❖ *The four fundamental motivations of life are desire, fear, duty, and love.*

- *Pain or suffering stems from desire or craving, the antidote for which is to cut the bonds of desire.*
- *Lasting happiness or joy is internal, whereas material gratification provides pleasure, which is external and transient.*
- *Worldly people are object-referred because they build their self-identity from material possessions like wealth, knowledge, relationships, and other accomplishments.*
- *Self-referral is the state where one derives joy from being in touch with their inner essence, which is not dependent on external factors or situations. It is happiness for no reason, unlike object referrals, which reflect happiness for some reason.*
- *The greatest obstacle to experiencing your inner reality, your very essence, is identification with your mind.*

4

THE SEVEN MIGHTY PRINCIPLES

Trainer: "In the last session, we discussed the 12th verse of Bhaja Govindam, which talks about the alternating dawn and dusk, day and night, summer and winter, etc., and the ebbing of life through this never-ending process of oscillation, to which the passing time stands perpetual witness. In this context, it would be enlightening to examine 'The Seven Mighty Principles' as they explain much of what Sri Sankara expounded in the illustrious poem.

Hermeticism is a mystical philosophy based on the writings attributed to Hermes Trismegistus, hailed as the father of science and founder of alchemy; alchemy ultimately became the art of chemistry, medicine, and virtually all of the modern sciences. Hermeticism offers profound insights into personal transformation and spiritual enlightenment.

Some Christian writers consider Hermes Trismegistus to be a wise pagan prophet who saw the coming of Christianity, while the Islamic tradition regards the Prophet to be a direct descendant of Hermes Trismegistus. Hermes, considered a contemporary of Abraham, developed much of what later became the basis for all esoteric teachings. "Hermetic Principles" can be found in both the most ancient of the Indian teachings and the scrolls of the ancient Egyptians.

Today much is written about Hermes, especially the Seven Principles he posited, which form the cornerstone of all knowledge. For more than a millennium, his teachings remained hidden. Their rediscovery by scholars who unearthed ancient manuscripts in the quest for age-old wisdom revived widespread interest in them, in the recent past.

The Seven Principles influence everything in the universe and are immutable. They are not subject to change, nor be questioned, modified, or destroyed. As Jose Silva of Mental Dynamics fame observed, they are like the rules of the road. Thanks to their universal application, they govern all things, from the smallest particle to the expanding universe. One can say that these principles are the rules of life.

Let's proceed to have a look at these Mighty Principles and see how Sankara's teachings have a bearing on them.

1) *The Principle of Mentalism*

The principle of mentalism states that the *universe is a creation of God.* It asserts that all is mind; the universe is mental. For anything to exist, a thought has to arise first, which then gets transformed into a physical reality or manifestation. This hypothesis gave rise to the theory of two creations propounded by modern management experts like Stephen R. Covey. 'Begin with the end in mind,' one of the seven habits of highly effective people evolved by Covey, is based on the principle that *all things are created twice.* There is a mental or first creation and a physical or second creation to all things.

Whether it is the construction of a home or starting a business, it is first created in the mind of the owner or entrepreneur, with every detail in proper perspective. Thereafter it gets reduced to a blueprint, and the construction plans or business plans are chalked out. The carpenter's rule "measure twice, cut once" is highly applicable in the first creation. You have to recheck and make sure that the blueprint, the first creation, is exactly what you want to achieve, or else it will cost you dearly during the second creation when the construction of the house starts or the business enterprise begins.

In Sanskrit, there is a saying: *"yadh/bhavam, thadh/bhavati"*. It means that whatever is conceived mentally, will get manifested physically. In other words, **what we think, we shall become. You do not attract what you want, but what you are. You get what you earn, not what you yearn for. Prayers are answered only when they are in harmony with your thoughts and deeds**.

You cannot choose your circumstance or situation, but you can choose your thoughts and influence your circumstance or situation surely enough, albeit indirectly. If we have the right thoughts, the right action will follow.

'CHANGE YOUR THOUGHTS AND YOU WILL CHANGE YOUR WORLD'

"Just as the characters in a novel are the creation of the novelist, we and everything else in the universe are a part of the Creator. We are parts of the totality of creation. Just as we are relative to God, so is our universe relative to us," observes Jose Silva.

Your world is the projection of your thoughts and is very much yours, just as my world is a mental creation of mine and is different from yours.

This principle can help us understand our minds better, and the *modus operandi* of its working. In Bhaja Govindam, Adi Sankara, directly and indirectly, emphasizes that the universe is a mental creation of God and that He alone is worthy of our glorification. Hence the Acharya emphasizes: *"Bhaja Govindam...... muda mate....."*

2) *Principle of Correspondence*

The second mighty principle states: *"As above, so below; as below, so above."* All things exist in the physical, mental, and spiritual planes. As is on the physical plane, so is on the mental plane; as is on the mental plane, so is on the spiritual plane. Just as the universe is a mental creation of God, so is your world a mental creation of your own.

Understanding this principle will help us unlock and tackle many emotions – positive and negative. Imagine that you have a victim's personality. When you go to a restaurant and are led to a table next to a swinging toilet door, or next to a person smoking a cigar, or a screaming baby, what do you do? If you take the seat grumbling something like, "There it is again; it's always like this for me," and such experiences happen to you more often than not, whether it be in a restaurant, department store, or a cinema theatre, you exhibit a victim's personality.

Is it possible to efface a victim's personality, and if so, how? Jose Silva says that we can, by applying the principle of correspondence. We can unlock the entire chain of victimization by working on the low end to unlock the high. Generally, a person who gets victimized in a minor way is the same person who gets victimized in a major way also. And the person who meekly accepts the unwanted seat at a restaurant is the same type of person who gets his or her house robbed. If we can end victimization in the simpler areas of life, we're well on the way to ending it in the more complex ones.

How to get over one's victimization? You go into a restaurant and you're led to a table you don't like. You call the host or hostess over and say, "Look. I do not like this table. Please let me have another." Chances are that in most instances, you'll get a better table. And, you are no longer a victim.

You go to a department store and purchase something that comes in a crushed box. You state, "Sorry, I don't like this box, it's damaged." In all likelihood, you will receive another good box.

But what if you don't get another table in the restaurant or a good box in the department store? You're still not a victim for the reason that you have asserted yourself. You have taken appropriate action rather than passively accepting the unacceptable. By asking for a better table or a good box, *you have set yourself up for a choice.*

You can remain in the restaurant or leave it, and the choice is yours only. You can accept the box at the department store or reject it, and again the choice is yours alone. If you are an assertive person, you might say something like, "Let me speak to your superior," and go on to the next echelon of customer service personnel. Look at the power of choice and assertiveness of doing so. Almost invariably, you will be able to speak with the person's immediate superior, and generally, if you have a genuine grievance, you will get things done the way you want."

Supriya: "Sir, one doubt. A person who has a victim's personality generally will not dare to question the decision of the restaurant or the department store in providing a lousy service. How then can he be expected to exercise his choice and confront the service provider by being assertive?"

Anandavardhan: "Assertive behavior does not mean that you bang on the table at the restaurant or pick up a quarrel at the department store. If you do that, it's called aggressive behavior, not assertive. The difference between the two is that assertive behavior assumes the life position: 'I'm O.K, you're O.K.,' which shows mutual respect and acceptance. Per contrast, aggressive behavior takes the assumption: 'I'm O.K., you are not O.K.' which attracts confrontation in the interaction.

An assertive person makes his demand courteously and with a smile and induces the other party to oblige the request. Although modest in words and actions, his demeanor conveys that he is conscious of his right to get proper service. With such a mindset, even a person with victim-personality also can exercise his choice and be assertive without any difficulty.

Once you use these methods for quite some time in daily life, you'll find that it's both refreshing and rewarding. When you realize that all people are operating in the same way – that is from their points of view – you begin to understand that everyone is right, as the first principle of mentalism expounds. Others are right because they believe they are right and for valid reasons from their perspective. But you know that you also are right from your viewpoint. When both are O.K. where is the scope to be angry or resentful about?

When this is understood, even a timid victim can turn to be assertive. This is because he knows that he is right and from that awareness, he draws a feeling of legitimacy that allows him to assert himself. At the same time, his awareness that others also consider themselves right allows him to be assertive without getting angry. And taking appropriate action when you feel you're about to be victimized makes you proactive, not reactive, and that helps to boost your self-image as well.

<u>MAJOR TAKEAWAYS</u>

- ❖ *Hermeticism is a mystical philosophy based on the writings of Hermes Trismegistus. It offers deep insights for personal transformation and spiritual enlightenment.*
- ❖ *Known as the seven mighty principles, these are immutable rules of life.*
- ❖ *The first principle states that the universe is a mental creation of God. Everything is created twice — the first is mental and the second is physical.*
- ❖ *What we think, we shall become.*

❖ *You get what you earn, not what you yearn for.*

❖ *The second mighty principle states: "As above, so below; as below, so above".*

❖ *Understanding this principle helps one unlock many emotions, both negative and positive. By applying it and adopting assertive behavior, one can overcome the victim mindset.*

❖ *Circumstances and situations may be beyond your control, but how to deal with them is within your control. You can exercise your choice and refuse to be a victim.*

5

THE SEVEN MIGHTY PRINCIPLES (Continued)

3) *The Principle of Vibration*

This principle states that *all things are in constant and never-ending motion. A change in the vibration causes a change in the manifestation. All* things in the universe are in motion – solid, liquid, or gas. The things move, vibrate, and travel in circular patterns. The only difference between one object and another is the rate of its vibration. And, each thing has its unique vibrational frequency, with which it is identified. Because of this, no two things in the universe are identical. Even solid objects like a rock or a desk also vibrate, albeit at a low frequency. On the other hand, your body vibrates at an extremely high rate.

Water at a high vibration is steam. At a low vibration, it turns to ice. But water, ice, and steam are the same, differing only in the vibration, which causes the change in its manifestation. The state of health has a vibration; so also illness. When you are ill, what is at the root of the problem is that your vibrations are not manifest. Healing is nothing but adjusting the vibrations to the proper level.

Our thoughts, emotions, and will send out vibrations into the universe. Every thought or mental state has a corresponding rate and mode of vibration. The vibrations emanating from us affect not only us but also the people around us. ***If we send out thoughts of envy, hatred, or jealousy, these will elicit the same thought patterns in others towards us.*** The point to note here is that we can choose our thoughts and emotions. Positive thoughts help us to progress towards spiritual development. And negative thoughts retard our progress or cause us to regress.

The law of Attraction operates by using our thoughts and feelings to dictate what we attract into our lives. Attraction is a force that acts mutually between particles of matter and tends to draw them together while resisting their separation. You cannot apply this law without understanding the law of vibration as these two are interconnected. As vibration is what causes attraction, we can conclude that the law of vibration is the primary law, and the other law is the secondary one.

The law of vibration always looks to match up people, things, and experiences. You can choose the law to match up with anything you want by deliberately choosing your vibrations. **You don't attract what you want; you attract who are. By changing your vibration, you can change your entire experience of the world.**

If we have negative thoughts, we will vibrate at a lower frequency. It can lead to feelings of anxiety, depression, and physical illness. On the other hand, if we have positive thoughts, we will vibrate at a higher frequency. This can lead to feelings of happiness, peace, and good health. *The bottom line is that by understanding the different frequencies of vibration, we can learn to control our thoughts and emotions and create the reality we desire*.

How the principle can be used to improve the quality of life

The following tips can help us harness the principle of vibration to our advantage.

- Be aware of your thoughts and emotions. Whenever these are negative, consciously try to replace them with positive thoughts and emotions. Eckhart Tolle says that 80 to 90 percent of most people's thinking is not only repetitive and useless, but because of its dysfunctional and often negative nature, much of it is also harmful. It causes a serious leakage of vital energy.

- Spend time in nature: Nature is full of high-frequency energy that can help you raise your vibrations. Go for a walk in the park or seashore, sit by a river, or listen to the sound of the ocean.

- Listen to the music that resonates with you.

- Practice meditation or yoga.

- Spend time with positive people. Remember the 9th verse of Bhaja Govindam that sings the glory of *satsanga* (association with positive-minded people).

- As Tolle suggests, make it a habit to monitor your mental-emotion state through self-observation. "Am I at ease at this moment?" is a good question to ask yourself frequently. Or, one can ask, "What's going on inside me at this moment?" If you get the inside right, the outside will fall into place.

"If you want to find the secrets of the universe, think in terms of energy, frequency, and vibration." (Nikola Tesla, the legendary inventor)

4) *The Principle of Polarity*

This mighty principle states that *all things are dual. Everything has its pair of opposites and these opposites are identical, differing only in degree.* For example, tall and short, although opposites, are the same. Everything has two poles, and everything has its opposite. There is hot and cold, light and dark, good and bad, etc. We cannot have one without the other.

In verse 12 of Bhaja Govindam, Sankara is reminding us about this principle operating constantly in nature: Day and night, morning and evening, winter and spring all come and go. While Time sports, life fleets unobserved. Yet the desire does not leave us, the Acharya laments.

"Polarity, or action and reaction, we meet in every part of nature; in darkness and light, in heat and cold, in the ebb and flow of waters, in male and female, in the inspiration and expiration of plants

and animals; in the equation of quantity and quality in the fluids of the animal body; in the systole and diastole of the human heart; in the centrifugal and centripetal gravity; in the electricity, galvanism and chemical affinity." (Ralph Waldo Emerson)

We use polarity to swing from one emotion to another, like from dislike to like, from fear to faith, hate to love, etc. As Jose Silva observes, it helps us to go from a sense of guilt to that of forgiving, and from anger to tolerance. When we hear words like love, fear, and anger, their meaning is better understood by examining the opposite of the given word. For example, consider the word fear. We know that it signifies a negative emotion. If you were to draw a scale of polarity with a negative on one end and a positive on the other, inarguably, you would place fear on the negative side.

On reflection, you would understand that it was an expectation to put fear on the negative side of the scale. Considering the nature of the word expectation, it could be placed at both ends of the scale, as expectation could be positive or negative. Fear is a negative expectation, whereas faith is a positive expectation. Therefore, fear and faith are the same, differing only by the degree of positivity or the degree of negativity. Change the degree and you change the emotion.

It can be seen that the principle of polarity gives us a clear concept of how transmutation and alchemy work. Transmutation is not changing one thing into a different thing at one go; it's changing the degree of the same thing. For example, we cannot transmute fear into love, but we can transmute fear into courage, or hate into love.

When we understand and use the principle of polarity, we gain a better insight into our mental state as it helps us to view our mental state in terms of the degree of a specific feeling, thought, or emotion. Accordingly, we can raise or lower our vibration at will and become masters of our vibration. This state frees us from the control of others' vibrations and ideals. To conclude, mastery of the principle of polarity enables us to perform physical, spiritual, and mental alchemy in all situations.

MAJOR TAKEAWAYS

- ❖ *The fifth mighty principle is the Principle of Vibration, which states that all things are in constant and never ending motion.*

- ❖ *A change in the vibration causes a corresponding change in the manifestation. We send vibrations of our thoughts, emotions, and will into the universe. We choose our thoughts and emotions.*

❖ *The Law of Attraction operates by using our thoughts and feelings to dictate what we attract into our lives.*

❖ *You don't attract what you want, but what you are.*

❖ *Some tips to harness the principle of vibration are discussed.*

❖ *The fourth principle, the Principle of Polarity, states that all things are dual. Everything has its pair of opposites.*

❖ *By using this principle, we can understand our mental state and manage our feelings, thoughts, and emotions suitably.*

6

THE SEVEN MIGHTY PRINCIPLES (Continued)

5) *The Principle of Rhythm*

This principle states that *everything flows out and in; everything has its tides; all things rise and fall; the pendulum swing manifests in everything; a measure of the swing to the right is a measure of the swing to the left; rhythm compensates.*

The principle shows that movement is characteristic of the universe, and the rhythm balances the changes between the polarities. All things show rise and fall. A rhythmic cycle marks the birth, growth, deterioration, and demise of everything. Look at the seasons that change from summer to winter, with autumn and spring in between. So also, the day and night, sunrise and sunset, the phases of the moon, the ebbs and the flow of the tides, and all other physical manifestations in the world display rhythmic movements.

You can see it in the human body, in the breathing out and breathing in, in the systole and diastole of the heart, in life and death. Rhythm is there in everything and everywhere. The principle also shows that nothing is ever permanent. Change is the only constant in an ever-changing life.

The principle of rhythm builds on the other Hermetic principles, especially the principle of vibration and the principle of polarity. This is the principle of change and it ensures that the movement is not random but equal in both directions of the pendulum. And, in most cases, these are measurable also.

How can one live with the principle of rhythm? As Sankaracharya says in the Bhaja Govindam, don't get attached to material possessions like wealth, knowledge, power, position, relationships, etc. Never get bonded to them; they all may disappear in the blink of an eye. Avoid emotional attachment to them; develop an indifferent attitude to the ebbs and flow of life, understanding that all things are transient.

As you cannot defy the laws of nature, wise it would be to go with the flow. When you see everything with the awareness that 'this too shall pass,' nothing should delight you beyond a limit, and nothing should worry you either. Because you know that it will be rhythmic, and you have little control over it.

Tips to live with the rhythm

- *<u>Be positive:</u>* As we discussed in the first principle, the crux of the Hermetic teachings is that everything is mental. It means that we create the reality of our lives from out of our thoughts and consciousness. The principle of mentalism says that ALL is the mind. It suggests that to live with the rhythm, we have to keep a positive mindset at all times – even when the pendulum swings to the opposite side.

<u>*Do not succumb to despair.*</u>

- When we understand the principle of polarity and that of rhythm, there is no reason for despair because we're sure that the pendulum will swing back to the other side.

- *<u>Persevere and be consistent.</u>* Do not be carried away by good times or get depressed when the tide turns unfavorable. Be consistent and move with the rhythm.

- *Don't bank on the ephemeral.* The Hermetic principles show that everything in life is subject to change, and nothing is permanent. Good health, youthfulness, relationships, wealth, and all the things in life are bound to be lost sooner or later, as asserted by Sri Sankara in the Bhaja Govindam. Understanding that the universe is a mental creation of God, learn to live with the rhythm of the creation.

- *Be grateful for the blessings of God.* When you are on cloud nine, be grateful to your creator and to the people who supported you in your endeavors. It will help you to cope better with the situations when the pendulum swings to the opposite side.

- *Be proactive and prepared for the inevitable lows.* Life has taught you that every stage in life will pass for its opposite. Be ready to live with the unfavorable swings of the pendulum by taking proactive steps to cope with the rhythm. Don't get depressed by the lows or elated by the highs in life.

6) *The Principle of Cause and Effect*

One day, long back, a leaf fell in a forest in California. It landed on the ground in front of a fat green caterpillar, which was inching along. It made a sharp deviation to avoid the obstacle on its path. Now, the caterpillar came to a log and crawled up its side. Just as it reached the top of the log, a man walking by came and sat on the log. And his weight squished the caterpillar. Suddenly, the man jumped up and felt the goo on the back of his pants.

He hurried back home, changed the clothes, and took the pants to the local laundry. There, he met a beautiful girl and started a conversation with her. He invited her for a coffee at the nearby café and spent some happy moments with her. They began to date, fell in love, and got married. A son was born to the couple. He grew up as a smart and intelligent boy and later became an attorney. The youngster went into politics and had a step-by-step rise in his party.

And so, because one day a leaf fell in a California forest, Richard Nixon became the thirty-seventh President of the United States-- cause and effect.

"Every cause has its Effect; every Effect has its Cause; everything happens according to Law; chance is but a name for Law not recognized; there are many planes of causation, but nothing escapes the Law." Thus goes the seventh mighty principle of cause and effect.

When something happens for which no cause is discernible, we attribute it to an accident. But there is nothing called accidents in Nature. Deepak Chopra puts it thus: "What we call *an accident* or a *random event* is the nonlocal correlation of the universal mind. Every event gets orchestrated by infinite consciousness, and every event is a conspiracy of an infinity of events. For anything to happen in your body, in your mind, in your life, the entire universe has to conspire."

As Deepak says, everything is connected with everything else, and if we are in sync with the universe, we can experience synchronicity. Every event in our life is being orchestrated by the entire universe. Nothing comes from nothing. If we cannot see a cause for an event, it does not mean that there's none; it only means that the cause is obscure and unknown. The law of cause and effect is nothing but the law of karma. It means that you are responsible for your life. Understanding this principle is gaining insight into the power of choice that is empowering.

These laws make us understand that ultimately life is in the hands of God, and being His creation, we have to surrender to Him. That is why Sankaracharya exhorts to sing the glory of the Almighty ("*Bhaja Govindam........muda mate*").

7) *The Principle of Gender*

This principle professes that *Gender is everything; everything has its masculine and feminine principles; gender manifests on all planes –physical, mental, and spiritual.*

The masculine force is the outgoing, the positive, and the instigative. On the other hand, the feminine force is incoming, receptive, negative, and creative. They have nothing to do with the male and female sexes. The sexes are just the manifestations of the principle of gender on the physical plane. Gender gets manifested in the mental and spiritual planes as well. For instance, a dynamic speaker, whether male or female, produces a masculine force in his/her speaking. Who's the masculine force in your life? Maybe your mother-in-law or your wife.

In the practical application of this principle, effective communication occurs when you speak with someone in the masculine or outgoing mode; when you're listening, you are in the receptive, the inflowing, the feminine mode. **Just as a magnet will attract another magnet only when its outgoing/ masculine pole is put together with the receptive/ feminine pole, so is communication.** If you were to speak from the receptive mode to a listener in the same mode, you would get a repelling force. Similarly, when you put the outgoing vis-a-vis the outgoing, again you have a repelling force. _For proper communication to occur, you must have positive with negative, receptive with the outgoing, the masculine with the feminine_.

When two people are eager to speak their minds, and both of them are in masculine mode, no communication would take place between them. The same thing happens when both of them are in receptive mode, and each wishes to hear the other person talking. The sender of the message should be, to some degree, in the masculine/outgoing mode and the receiver in the feminine/receptive mode for any sharing of meaning to be effective. The absence of this is a major reason for many communication failures.

One can find this principle in operation in all walks of life and all endeavors – in writing, painting and other forms of arts, sports, business, and all professions. You only have to be aware of its existence to locate this force. There are salespeople, attorneys, stockbrokers, doctors, politicians, and co-workers who can induce you to do something without any demur. It is a display of their charisma, and charisma is a strong outgoing/masculine force. All great speakers and motivators possess it.

All forceful people are outgoing. Authority figures mostly are seen as masculine figures, and you tend to switch to the receptive mode in their presence. An understanding of the principle of gender will help you exercise your freedom and power to choose your response (the masculine and feminine forces within yourself) and take better charge of your life to be an able communicator.

Concluding remarks

If you reflect on and work with the seven mighty principles discussed here, they can help you lead a rich and rewarding life. Their usefulness in life will unfold as you continue to grow and evolve. These principles are the rules of life. Many of them resonate well with the expositions of Adi Sankara in the Bhaja Govindam, like the universe is the creation of God, everything is mental; as above, so below, as below, so above; all things are dual; all things have their tides, an ebb tide as well as a flood tide, and every cause has its effect and vice versa. For instance, by learning to become more and more assertive in daily life, you can choose not to become a victim and get exploited; by gaining a better understanding of the cause and effect, one can create new cause by setting meaningful goals; using polarity, you can change from the negative to the positive, from fear to faith, from hate to love, etc.

❖ *The fifth mighty principle states that everything follows a rhythm – flowing out and in, rising and falling, swinging to the right and the left.*

❖ *Change is the only constant in an ever-changing life; and rhythm is the principle of change.*

❖ *Everything in life being rhythmic, do not get attached to anything.*

❖ *The sixth principle states that every cause has an effect, and every effect, its cause.*

❖ *Chance is a name for the Law not recognized. What is called an accident is the non-local correlation of the universal mind.*

❖ *The seventh and the last Hermetic Principle postulates that Gender is everything; everything has its masculine and feminine principles.*

❖ *This principle is in operation in all walks of life and all endeavors.*

❖ *An understanding of the principle of gender will help us exercise our freedom and power to choose our responses, and to take better charge of our life.*

❖ *Many of the seven mighty principles resonate well with the expositions of Adi Sankara in the 'Bhaja Govindam'.*

7

CHOOSE THE PATH OF 'SHREYAS'

Trainer: "According to the Vedas, there are two paths in human life – the path of *shreyas* and the path of *preyas*. People are generally attracted to the path of *preyas* as they find pleasure, fame, name, power, position, and the like in pursuing it. These outcomes stem from the ego and are transitory. On the contrary, the path of *shreyas* leads to the ultimate good and is the one that enlightens and enriches life forever."

Sandeep: "Then, why do people choose the path of preyas?"

Trainer: "That shows the overriding influence of one's *sanskara* and *vasana* accumulated over lifetimes. We will discuss them shortly. Before that, let's move to the next verse of *Bhaja Govindam*. It says:

Ka/te/kantha/dhanagatachinta

Vatula/kim/tava/nasti/niyanta

Trijagati/sajjanasangatireka

Bhavati/bhavarnavatarane/nauka(13)

"Oh, distracted one! Why do you worry about your wife, wealth......? Is there not for you the one who ordains? In the three worlds, only the association with wise people can serve as a boat to cross the sea of *samsara* (so, seek Govinda, seek Govinda)."

The Acharya asks: "Why do you worry about your wife and wealth?" Here, the word wife stands for all your relationships in life, and wealth refers to all the material possessions. In worrying, there is a leakage of energies, because of which overflowing is rendered impossible. One can be filled with the mystery of the Divine only when the energies overflow. And, this can be made possible when there's no worry.

Worry means a lack of trust in God and is tantamount to an insult to God's wisdom and benevolence. Over to a story: A couple was crossing a river in a boat. When they reached the middle of the overflowing river, there came a storm. The wife was suddenly filled with panic, whereas the husband appeared calm and serene. The lady started screaming and asked her man: "Are you not scared that we may get drowned soon?"

"No," said the husband. He suddenly pulled out a sharp knife from his bag and yelled at her: "I'm going to kill you, right now."

The wife was not perturbed at the threat of her husband. She remained calm in front of the knife pointed at her. He asked her why she was not scared by his words. She said: "The knife can kill me, I know. But the one who wields it is my loving husband. So, why should I worry?"

The husband said, "The same logic holds good in the situation we're encountering now. The waves may be turbulent, but the Lord who wields the waves loves you and me; why should we be scared? Have unqualified faith in God. To doubt God's powers or intention is to mistrust Him."

Such an unwavering faith in God at all times makes a person truly spiritual. The creator cares for the created, he believes.

Supriya: "But, is it not natural for common people to worry in such situations in life?"

Trainer: "People start to worry because they misinterpret suffering as misery. The problem is the wrong interpretation. Suffering is to be reckoned as a gift from the Divine. The Buddha says that pain or suffering arises from desire or craving and that to be free of pain, we need to cut the bonds of desire. Suffering is to be taken as a wake-up call of existence for us to come out of the sleepy consciousness. For this purpose, Sri Sankara suggests *satsanga* – association with good people—as the only way out. If you are in the company of wise people who are balanced and tranquil, you'll learn to remove the reckless craving and unnecessary worry from the mind.

Sankara asks: "Why are you worried about a transitory connection with your wife of a single life? In the endless eternity of life after life, is this just not a fleeting moment? Once you are dead and gone, what is the connection between you and your wife of today? And when this is the case with the life partner, what to say about your wealth and other material acquisitions? What happens to them once you're gone? Why, then, should you engage in such profitless thoughts?"

Satsanga

The seeds of the tendencies or *vasanas*, carried over from past lives and lying dormant in the *jiva,* are waiting for the right time and environment to sprout and grow within all of us. Depending on the company we keep, these latent tendencies germinate and come to fruition, just like the seeds of plants sprout in the right climatic conditions.

This explains why it is supremely important to mix with good people. We do not know the type of seeds (of tendencies) lying dormant within us. If we mix with people with bad habits, lower values, or principles, the latent seeds of negative tendencies we carry in our consciousness germinate and grow as our bad habits.

Experts say that if you keep doing a thing continuously for 21 days, it becomes your habit. And if you continue to do it for 21 days more, that habit becomes your lifestyle.

Each of your habits creates a specific 'groove' or pathway in your brain. These patterns induce you to behave in a particular manner, perhaps even against your wish. Your life follows these grooves. But there is a flip side to this phenomenon. You can neutralize the dictates of any bad habit by creating brain patterns of good habits. Furthermore, you can completely erase the brain grooves of bad habits by doing meditation. There is no other way, says Paramhamsa Yogananda.

However, you cannot cultivate good habits without keeping good company and a facilitative environment.

Satsanga, or association with good people, helps us to make a paradigm shift in our thinking. Earlier, in the first Hermetic Principle, we found that *everything is mental.* Control of senses (*dhama)* leads to mental peace (*sama*). It is this *sama* that nourishes happiness in the heart (joy). Once the internal state is of peace and joy, the thought process will get attuned to achieving inner purity. Remember, all this is rendered possible thanks to the association with people who tread the path of righteousness through noble thoughts and deeds. That is why Sankara says that *satsanga* serves as a boat to cross the sea of change. It protects the *saadhak (seeker of truth)* from the onslaught of the negative tendencies accumulated in the *jiva* over the past lives.

In the second line of the verse under discussion, the Acharya asks: *"Vatula/kim/tava/nasti/niyanta...."* which means 'is there not for you the one who ordains?' (so, why do you worry?)

There is a story about Sant Kabir, the Sufi poet. He was very poor but had a large number of followers. Some people, who were envious of the poet's popularity, wanted to insult him, and they chalked out a devious plan for the purpose. They spread a rumor across the village and beyond, which said that Kabir intended to host a feast on a particular day at a given place and that he welcomed all to partake of the food. The news spread like wildfire, even in the adjacent villages.

Kabir also got to know that someone was organizing a feast for all. Without knowing that it was the handiwork of his distractors, the poet also went to the function on the appointed date. The well-wishers and followers of Kabir, who came to know about the event, thought: "What a magnanimous gesture on the part of the holy man to feed everyone. Considering that he is of poor means, we should all contribute generously to the effort taken by the master." This message also spread everywhere. As a result, the people who went to the feast also carried a lot of fruits, cooked food, and other edible materials, as a mark of their respect for the Sufi master.

Resultantly, all those who assembled at the venue got a sumptuous meal. The followers of Kabir enthusiastically arranged and distributed all the food items poured in from different areas. Kabir also happily partook in the offering; the people who assembled and participated in the feast thought that it was an act of charity by the Sufi master.

All that happens in the universe has a cause behind it, as we have seen in the Hermetic principles discussed earlier. The jealous people in the Kabir's story wanted to humiliate and insult him, but their attempt was thwarted promptly by the creator. Sri Sankara tells us in the verse not to get overworked on worldly issues and to repose full faith and trust in the ordainer, the Almighty.

With this 13th verse of *Bhaja Govindam,* the *dwadashamanjarikastotram* (a bouquet of 12 flowers), believed to have been compiled and sung by Adi Sankara, comes to an end. The subsequent 14 verses have been contributed to the poem by his 14 disciples who were with the master on the occasion.

MAJOR TAKEAWAYS

❖ *An unwavering faith in God makes a person truly spiritual.*

❖ *According to the Buddha, pain or suffering arises out of desire or craving for something.*

❖ *Suffering is a wake-up call of the Divine to bring us out of our sleepy consciousness.*

❖ *Depending on the company one keeps, the latent tendencies within the person germinate and grow. This shows the importance of 'satsanga.'*

❖ *If you do a thing continuously for 21 days, it becomes your habit; do it for 21 more days without a break, and it becomes your lifestyle.*

8

THE SELF-CENTERED PSEUDO-SAINTS

Whereas Sri Sankara composed and sang the first 13 slokas (verses) of *Bhaja Govindam,* including the first verse, which is a chorus and gets repeated at the end of all the other *slokas,* the subsequent 14 verses were each contributed by the Acharya's 14 disciples, who were with the master on the occasion and got inspired by the latter's rendition. These verses came to be known as *Chaturdasamanjarika stotram* (a bouquet of 14 flowers).

It is believed that the 14th *sloka* was compiled by the Acharya's foremost disciple, Padmapadar. It goes as under:

Jatilo/mundi/lunchitakesa

Kashayambarabahukritavesha

Pasyannapi/ca/na /pasyati /mudho

Hyudaranimittam/bahukritavesham (14)

"One (ascetic) with hair locks, another with head shaven, yet another with hair pulled out one by one, and also wearing saffron robes – these are fools who, though seeing, do not see. The different disguises are just for filling their belly. Seek Govinda.....seek Govinda...."

This verse ridicules and rebukes the pseudo-sannyasins who, without understanding the real significance of sannyasa, put on external marks like a shaven head, matted hair, pulled-out hair, or ochre robe to mislead people and gain undue advantage. Their only purpose is to fill the belly. Is this Sannyasa?

Although the direct reference in this verse is to pseudo-sannyasins, such types of hypocrites are aplenty in every walk of life, especially in the modern age. They include political leaders, administrators, priest class, etc. If an ordinary person leads a duplicitous life, maybe people in his inner circle alone will suffer, whereas if an administrator or a political leader resorts to such deceitful tactics, its harmful impact will have wider ramifications.

Sannyasa decoded

In Sanskrit, sannyasa means renunciation of action. It presupposes a performance of action to be renounced. First of all, there should be something you are doing right now that you want to abdicate. Is it possible to renounce something that you don't possess or are not doing? If you are not satisfied with your life because you have not been able to fulfill your ambitions and aspirations, and you choose to keep aloof from such a life, can it be called renunciation?

In the Bhagavad Gita, Krishna says:

Kamyanaam/karmanam/nyasam/sanyasam/kavayovidhuh

Sarvakarmaphalatyagam/prahustyagam/vichakshnah

(18.2)

"The Sages understand sannyasa to be the renunciation of work with desire; the wise declare the abandonment of the fruits of all actions as TYAGA."

Renunciation is "totally giving up all desire-prompted activities," and abandonment is "giving up all anxieties for enjoying the fruits of action." To the uninitiated, both these terms may appear to be the same. Admittedly, 'abandonment' has an integral relationship with 'renunciation." However, there is a subtle difference between tyaga and sannyasa. The action happens in the present, whereas its desired fruit belongs to the future. The anxiety regarding the fate of the action and the desire to enjoy the fruit thereof create a disturbance in our mind regarding a FUTURE period.

Both the desire and the agitation bring about restlessness. The deeper the desire, the greater the dissipation of one's inner energy. Unless our clinging attachment to the desired fruits of actions is abandoned (sacrificed through *tyaga*), we will not tap into the full potentialities of our personality. Without such abandonment of the attachments, our activities are bound to become ineffective, and ineffective activities can never fetch us enjoyable fruits.

To put it differently, 'Renunciation' is the goal to be achieved through the process of 'Abandonment' of our continuing anxiety to enjoy the fruits of actions. In short, 'Abandonment' *(Tyaga)* is the means to reach the goal of 'Renunciation' (*Sannyasa*). Both aspects are integral parts of our moment-to-moment activities, and neither suggests abdicating work. On the other hand, it implies that WORK WE MUST, at all costs. But, without being saddled by desires and hustled by anxieties, both of which are debilitating.

The verse under discussion asserts that renouncing is not a matter of external show. It is a victory that has to be earned within. When the heart is full of burning desires, the external signs of a shaven head, long matted hair, or other physical features of 'renunciation' are meaningless and deceptive.

Tiruvalluvar said, "There is no need for shaving the head or long-matted locks if what the world condemns is given up sincerely."

The need for survival is a living being's basic need; for a man, it's the lowest need. The need for enlightenment is the highest. Manipulative people who resort to dressing up like monks are seeking to fulfill their survival needs by adopting unethical means. Some so-called spiritual leaders create pomp and mysticism around them. Some appease rich people, satisfy their ego, and fulfill their need for survival.

UNENDING DESIRES

Over to the next stanza. It is attributed to Totakacharya.

Angam/galitam/palitam/mundam

Dasanavihinam/jatam/tundam

Vrddho/yati/grhitva/dandam

Tadapi/na/muncatyasapindam (15)

'The body has worn out; the head has turned all grey; the mouth has lost all teeth. The man goes about leaning on a staff. Still, he leaves not his bundle of desires.'

The focus of this verse is on the unending human desires. Man dies, but not his desires. No sooner than one desire gets fulfilled, another one will crop up. Life is a circle with a center and a periphery. Most of us live in the periphery and seek material pursuits and relationships. Seldom would we look into the center of life and seek answers to questions like "Who am I?" or "What is the purpose and meaning of my life?" Our life revolves around desires, attachments, and disappointments. When we look into ourselves and gain knowledge about the Self, we learn to give up our desires and become more and more receptive to the Lord's overflowing grace.

Osho's definition of freedom from desire is "to be free, totally free, to have or not to have desires. Desire should not be an obsession- that is the meaning." For example, your friend constructs a beautiful house, and a desire arises in your mind to have a house like that. Now, are you free to have the desire or not? If you are free, you are desire-less. On the contrary, if the desire to possess such a house persists and haunts you, you are not free and are attached and bonded. If you allow desires to be your masters, you turn a victim. And you will suffer much because there are millions of things going around, and if so many desires take possession of you, you will get torn apart.

The equation for eternal happiness

Happiness can be depicted as a mathematical equation $H=R/N$, where the 'H' stands for happiness/contentment, 'R' for the resources at your command, and the 'N' for your needs or desires. As your needs or desires go down, the 'H' quotient increases. If the 'N' factor could be brought down to nil, the 'H' reaches infinity.

As one advances in old age, the resources at his disposal decrease drastically, including the physical, mental, and financial. But the irony is that his needs or desires refuse to move in tandem with the depleting resources, which leads to despair and agitation. George Bernard Shaw said, "Man has to face two tragedies in life, one when his desire is fulfilled and the other, when it is not." In both cases, he ultimately faces mental agitation – one early and the other, later.

True happiness does not belong to the realms of the physical, emotional, or intellectual. Our Real Self lies beyond all these levels, and it is the only source of infinite happiness. Christ said, "The kingdom of heaven lies within you. He who knoweth shall find it."

Guru Nanak said the same thing when he said, "If you want permanent happiness, seek the Ram within you." In the *Bhaja Govindam,* Adi Sankara says, "Seek Govinda, seek Govinda, for He alone can provide eternal happiness."

Desires and the Karmic Law

The karmic law requires that every human wish find ultimate fulfillment, says Paramahamsa Yogananda. ***Desire is thus the chain that binds man to the reincarnation wheel. The mere presence of a body signifies that its existence is rendered possible by unfulfilled desires***. In *Autobiography of a Yogi*, Sri Yukteswar, Yogananda's guru, who resurrected in front of the *sishya,* said, "So long as the soul of man is encased in one, two, or three body containers, sealed tightly with the corks of ignorance and desires, he cannot merge with the sea of Spirit. When the gross physical receptacle is destroyed by the hammer of death, the other two coverings — astral and causal — remain to prevent the soul from consciously joining the Omnipresent Life. When desirelessness is attained through wisdom, its power disintegrates the two remaining vessels. The tiny human soul emerges, free at last; it is one with the Measureless Amplitude."

Totakacharya, in the stanza under discussion, bewails that people do not give up desires even when age has rendered them incapable of enjoying anything. See how realistically the picture of progressing from youth to old age is depicted: once old age sets in, the organs degenerate (*angam/galitam)*, then the hair turns grey (*palitam/mundam)*, the mouth becomes toothless (*dasanavihitam /jatam/tundam)*; what's more, unable to even stand upright without support, he manages to do so with the help of staff (*vriddho/yati/ grihitva/ dandam)*. Still, his desires remain strong as in the younger age. And these desires leave him not, even when he dies. The unfulfilled desires are the cause of his reincarnation

MAJOR TAKEAWAYS

* ❖ *There are cheats and frauds amongst sannyasins. They put on external signs of the renouncers and roam everywhere, just to hoodwink people and fill their bellies.*

* ❖ *Such hypocrites can be found in any walk of life in the society.*

* ❖ *According to Lord Krishna, 'sannyasa' is the renunciation of work with desire; 'tyaga' is the abandonment of the fruits of all actions.*

❖ *Desire and agitation cause restlessness. The deeper the desires, the greater the dissipation of inner energy.*

❖ *Renunciation is the goal to be achieved, and abandonment of the anxiety for the fruits of actions is the means to realize that.*

❖ *Desire should never become an obsession, lest you should be doomed.*

❖ *Happiness can be expressed as an equation, H=R/N, where 'H' stands for happiness, 'R' for the resources at command, and 'N' for the needs or desires.*

❖ *Desire is the chain that binds man to the reincarnation wheel. Unfulfilled desires at the time of death cause the rebirth.*

9

THE SELF-DELUDED HYPOCRITE

The previous *sloka* of 'Bhaja Govindam' showed how a householder could be under the tyranny of desires. The next verse, believed to have been composed and sung by Hastamalak, another disciple of Sankaracharya, shows how even a monk could be a victim of desires.

Agre/vahnih/prushte/bhanuh

Ratrau/chubukasamarpitajanuh

Karatalabhikshastarulatavasah

Tadapi/na/munchatyasapasah (16)

In front, there is fire; at his back, the sun; late at night, he sits with his knees held to his chin; he receives alms in his scooped palm and lives under the shelter of some tree; yet the noose of desires spare him not. (Seek Govinda, seek Govinda.....)

In Bhagavad Gita (3.6), the Lord says: One may appear to be physically retired from worldly matters. But if it is not accompanied effectively by an equal measure of mental and intellectual withdrawal from the sensuous fields, he is a misinformed seeker with bleak prospects.

As the first Hermetic principle posits, everything is mental. The mind tends to repeat its thoughts. If it constantly meditates on sensual pleasures, the mind develops a deep sensuous tendency, and the person leads a life that seeks fulfillment of his desires. Externally displaying the signs of morality and ethics but internally treading a life of low motives and foul sentiments is certainly not characteristic of a spiritual seeker but a self-deluded hypocrite!

Usually, people aspire to fame, name, power, position, respectability, etc. Even a monk, many a time, is caught up in a desire to be respected and appreciated, and he eventually gets trapped in that bondage.

Once a desire erupts in the mind, you cannot remove it, even if you try. Fighting with desire is like fighting with darkness. The only way to take on darkness is to bring a light to dispel it-- the light of knowledge and wisdom. So, the Acharya suggests: "Bhaja Govindam, bhaja Govindam."

The verse under review draws the picture of a monk who is outwardly simple and humble. But internally, he is filled with desires, which shows he is bonded and is not free. Externally, he may be non-violent and peaceful, but with burning desires inside, he is agitated and violent within. Spirituality is the way to gain victory over terrorizing desires that spell man's doom. The subjugation of the binding passions and victory of the soul will be possible only by invoking the blessings of the Almighty. So, the master suggests: seek refuge in Him. Only a person who surrenders to God has spiritual power. When you surrender at the feet of the Almighty, you will be internally free of your desires.

According to Jiddu Krishnamurti, "a disciplined mind is never a free mind, nor can a mind that has suppressed desire ever be free. It is only through understanding the process of desire the mind can be free. The mind that is limited by envy, by the 'me', the acquisitive desire for things, or virtue can never be truly religious. The religious mind is not a comparative mind. The religious mind sees and understands the full significance of what is."

Rituals and knowledge

"Kurute/gangasagaragamanam

Vrithaparipalanamathava/daanam

Jnanaviheenah/sarvamatena

Muktim/na/bhajati/janmasatena"   (17)

'One may go on pilgrimage, observe vows, and give away wealth in charity. Yet, devoid of the knowledge of the Self, nothing can give him freedom even in 100 lifetimes.'

'Kurute/gangasagaragamanam' – he goes to Gangasagar on pilgrimage. Gangasagar is a place in Kolkata in eastern India where the river Ganga meets the ocean. It is a very holy place. 'Ganga' also stands for the north, which means he may go to Kasi, the Himalayas, or Rishikesh for pilgrimage. 'Sagara' stands for the south, meaning holy places in the south like Rameswaram. The term *gangasagaragamanam* thus refers to one going to the holy places in the north and the south on pilgrimage.

The observances of pilgrimage, vows, and charity mark the lives of sincere spiritual seekers. The above stanza tells that even if we meticulously follow all these things, devoid of *jnana*- knowledge- *bhajati/ na/ muktim/janmasatena* –even after 100 lifetimes, we will not achieve liberation or *mukti*.

Malathi: "Does it mean that all the spiritual practices the seekers follow are superfluous and worthless, Sir?"

Trainer: "Not really. They are all needed. All these spiritual practices are essential for self-purification. And self-purification is an absolute requirement for gaining knowledge, not a substitute for knowledge to gain deliverance. In other words, mere purification is not an end in itself. All the said practices are only the means to the end, called the realization of liberation through knowledge.

The Vedas have two portions – the ritualistic or *karma kanda,* and the knowledge-centric or *jnana kanda.* All the ritualistic portions lead to discipline, but it is not to be reckoned as the 'be all and end all' of the total understanding. Rituals unless backed with understanding and knowledge are worthless.

Rituals are secondary practices equipping one with discipline, faith, patience, and detachment, which are essential for the purification of the mind. However, the primary practice is true wisdom, the knowledge of the Self. In the previous verse (No 16), Hastamalak pooh-poohed the vain austerity measures of the monks, who get mired in the vortex of unending desires within. The same idea is expanded further in the present *sloka*, which is attributed to Subodhacharya, another disciple of Sankaracharya.

The householders, treading the path of spirituality, go on pilgrimages, undertake vows, do charitable activities, etc. under the impression that these measures will take them to God. They fail to understand that such steps, unless supported by the acquisition of knowledge of the Ultimate, serve little purpose in the end. *Srutis* repeatedly point out *"jnanam / vina / moksho / na / siddhyate "* (without knowledge, liberation is impossible to realize). Subodhacharya also says, *"jnanavihinah/ muktim/na/bhajati"*   (without *jnana, mukti* remains unattained); even if 100 such lives pass by."

The state of an enlightened person

We are all driven by ego, which constitutes a false personality. Ego thrives on pretense, recognition, awards, rewards, accolades, etc., and craves to be on the top always. The most common ego identifications have to do with possessions, the work you do, social status, recognitions, etc., writes Eckhart Tolle. This state arises from vanity and a lack of real knowledge. This is what Subodhacharya calls *"Jnanavihinah."*

Chanakya Neeti portrays the state of an enlightened person thus:

"Egoism gets dissolved

In the knowledge of the Supreme Soul

Then, wherever the mind goes

There it meets the Ultimate Goal" (2.10)

When the Ultimate knowledge called *atma vidya* gets awakened in a person, he becomes enlightened, and his ego vanishes. Such a person is free and is not dependent on anything else for happiness. He is content with himself. He thinks differently. Such a mind can perceive God everywhere and in everything. Call it the state of true self-realization.

Most of the complications in life arise from one's ego. So, shed your ego and see how uncomplicated the life becomes. To enjoy the happiness of being in the moment – which is, what matters the most –one needs to have an ego-free mind. As long as the egoistic mind is running your life, you cannot be at ease; you cannot be at peace or fulfilled.

- *Everything is mental; if the mind constantly meditates on sensual pleasures, the person will lead a life that seeks the fulfillment of desires.*

- *Fighting a desire is like fighting darkness. Only a light can get the darkness dispelled. In life, the darkness of ignorance can be dispelled only by the light of knowledge.*

- *The Vedas comprise two portions; one is ritualistic, and the other is knowledge-centered. Rituals constitute secondary practice. The primary practice is true wisdom – the knowledge of the Self.*

- *An enlightened person has gained the Ultimate Knowledge – atma vidya.*

- *Most complications in life are created by ego. Life becomes uncomplicated for the person who sheds his ego.*

10

A MAN OF STEADY WISDOM

In the previous *slokas*, we found the characteristics of a self-deluded saint and a misguided householder who believed that by the mere show of austerity or by pursuing the path of rituals, one could reach God. Going ahead, in the next verse, Sureshwaracharya, another disciple of Adi Sankara, describes how a truly detached yogi behaves and lives.

"Surumandiratarumulanivasah

Sayya/bhutalamajinam/vasah

Sarvaparigrahabhogatyagah

Kasya/sukham/na/karoti/viragah" (18)

'He resides in some temple or beneath a tree. Earth is his mattress, and a deerskin is his robe. Who will not be happy upon giving up all the comforts of life? Detachment (*vairagya*) showers happiness (*sukha*) upon everyone.'

An increase in desires only brings pain and sorrow. A man of wisdom has successfully cast away all desires from his mind. A man of ignorance considers himself the ego, owing to which he has a burning desire to sense objects. To escape from the clutches of desires and attachments is no ordinary task. One who has succeeded in it will be free from external pomp or show of any kind because he has subdued his ego.

In the Bhagavad Gita (2.55), the Lord describes a man who has transcended his ego as a man of steady wisdom. He is self-satisfied in the Self and will not need to entertain any desires. According to Sankaracharya, a man of steady wisdom is not affected by the three calamities faced by ordinary people, viz. *adhyatmika, adhibhautika,* and *adhidaivika.* The first of these three refers to problems arising from the disorders of the body. The second type of calamity arises from external objects such as wild animals. And the third, those arising from causes brought in by natural forces like floods, storms, etc. Little wonder that such a person can sleep in the open under a tree, on the bare ground, wearing a deerskin, and renouncing all ideas of possession and longing to enjoy.

Sannyasa doesn't mean one has to renounce the world at large. It will be an absurd idea. One can only give up the attachment and infatuation to the world. That is what Christ meant when he counseled, "Be in the world but not of it."

It is said that in ancient Tibet, there was a religious practice that proclaimed the importance of not getting attached to anything. During the celebration of a particular festival, they would create a *Yantra,* a mystical symbol in a temple. The whole monastery would get involved in its creation, which called for a complex calculation and required many days of meticulous work for its flawless completion. And what would they do with the *Yantra* created so painstakingly by so many people? After the prayers are over and the celebration is completed, the Yantra will be wiped off!

Just imagine. Something that was made taking so much care, pain, and meticulous calculation is simply erased in a few moments, once the purpose is over. Symbolically, it suggests that we should not be attached to anything. Letting go should be the attitude adopted in life

Tiruvalluvar said, "There is no possession as great as non-desire, either in this world or in the worlds beyond." One should not let one's mind get tossed about in quest of desires, which only bring unhappiness. Happiness is an internal state of mind that requires no external objects to generate or sustain it.

After all, why one should chase desires? Chanakya Neeti says:

"Desires of the mind!

Who has got all the cushy things?

Everything depends on destiny

Therefore, count your blessings." (2.9)

The mind is very tricky; as soon as you fulfill one desire, another will crop up. You may have everything you want, yet a new desire will always crop up. According to Chanakya, everything you have is yours because of your destiny. What you are destined to get will surely come to you, unasked.

Instead of building upon your desires, which never will end, you should count your blessings. Be happy and content with what you have. Leave the rest to your destiny.

Sandeep: "Sir, one doubt. Is this proposition of Chanakya not a fatalistic one, encouraging people to sit idle with no ambition or desire, and wait for destiny to bring whatever is due to them?"

Trainer: "It has to be interpreted differently, Sandeep. As Swami Chinmayananda observed, "philosophy is not a subject that can be rightly understood by hasty students." In the Bhagavad Gita, Lord Krishna says. "Thy right is to work only, but never to its fruits; let the fruit-of-action be not thy motive, nor let thy attachment be to inaction (2.47)". Karma Yoga posits that since you have got a body, you cannot resort to inaction. Period.

The indoctrination in the Gita is that if success is what you seek, then never strive with a mind dissipated with anxieties and fears about the fruits of your action. For instance, suppose a farmer, for fear of failure of his crops due to possible adverse climatic conditions, fails to plow and sow at the right time, he is guaranteed to fail in farming. The power of NOW is such that nothing will ever happen in the future; it will always happen in the NOW. So, it calls for investing intelligently in the present moments. Therefore, to worry and get anxious about the future rewards of our present actions, simply serves to escape from the dynamic PRESENT moment and live in the FUTURE moment that is not yet born!

In short, the Gita-stanza mentioned here gives four injunctions while guiding us to be true workers, writes Chimayananda: 'A real *Karma Yogin* understands that (i) his concern is with action alone; (ii) he has no concern with results; (iii) he should not entertain the motive of gaining a fixed (specific) fruit for a given action; and (iv) these ideas do not mean that he should sit back courting inaction.' I think Sandeep got his doubt clarified."

Your destiny is what you create by dedicated and desireless actions that you perform in life. Simplicity, bare minimum possessions, and total dispassion are the mantras for success in spiritual life and the source of eternal happiness.

The Goal Supreme

Nityananda, another disciple of Sankara, composed the 19th *sloka* of *Bhaja Govindam*, which goes as:

"Yogarato/va/bhogarato/va

Sangarato/va/sangavihinah

Yasya/Brahmani/remate/chittam

Nandati/nandati/nandatyeva"   (19)

'Let one revel in yoga or bhoga. Let one seek enjoyment in company or solitude. He whose mind revels in Brahman, he enjoys; he alone enjoys. Seek Govinda, seek Govinda.....'

Spiritual evolution that makes one seek, find, and revel in Brahman is not achieved thanks to the efforts made in just one lifetime. It is the outcome of the person's endeavors and attainments in the past lives, which are "enduringly retained in the astral brain," says Paramahansa Yogananda. Like seeds, these astral retentions germinate when the conditions are right. What triggers a 'right condition' may be almost anything. Sri Ramakrishna, the great master who lived in Bengal, India, in the nineteenth century, had his first spiritual awakening as a child on beholding a flock of cranes flying in graceful beauty against a gray sky!

As Swami Chinmayananda writes in his interpretation of Bhagavad Gita (6.44), each birth has a logical continuity with its past, as strictly as we experience in day-to-day life. It is like a statement of account (SoA) issued by a bank. The debit, credit, and balance columns in the SoA reflect what we have withdrawn, deposited, and retained as balance in the account during the statement period. Similarly, the cultural growth of a given mind and intellect is carried over from the account of the previous births and brought forward to the current account of the current birth.

A man who had in the past lived a life of self-control, study, and practice will exhibit those cultural traits in his present life, instinctively. ***Each one of us has an instinctive bend of mind, and we get irresistibly drawn towards it.*** This pull is most powerful when arising from our essential evolutionary tendencies, points out Chinmayananda. For instance, Swami cites, "Even a bandit chieftain can, overnight, turn himself to be a determined seeker, and, ere long, become a great poet of the land, as Valmiki did in the past." Any number of such examples could be drawn from our recent history and in the present times. In all those cases, "the only satisfactory explanation will be that the individual mind and intellect was expressing through its given physical structure its characteristic tendencies, which it had acquired by itself in its past incarnations, through its willful actions and deliberate motives."

Gautama Buddha used to say, "You should be like a house which has light inside. When the house, its doors, and its windows are showing light, thieves don't come close. But when the house is dark, and there is no light, it is an opportunity for thieves." "......Arrogance, ego, aggressiveness, superiority, the idea of being special – all are destroying you and your peace."

In the carnal world, a man thinks of objects, and attachment arises. From attachment, desire is born, which eventually causes anger (Gita, 2.62). Anger progressively leads to delusion, loss of memory, destruction of discrimination, and the final fall (ibid, 2.63). A deluded mind can never see the timeless Brahman. By saying that the house should be fully lit so that the thieves would keep away, Buddha was suggesting that we should seek enlightenment, which, by itself, would ward off all the 'thieves.'

<u>MAJOR TAKEAWAYS</u>

- ❖ *A man of steady wisdom has transcended his ego. Ego attracts desires; wisdom dispels them.*
- ❖ *A man of steady wisdom is not affected by the three calamities, viz. 'adhyatmika', 'adibhautika', and 'adidaivika'*
- ❖ *Be happy and contented with what you have; leave the rest to destiny.*
- ❖ *Your destiny is created by you when you do your karma without being anxious about its fruits.*

- ❖ *Cultural and spiritual attainments are enduringly retained in the astral brain of the individual.*
- ❖ *Each birth has a logical continuity with its past. The cultural evolution of a given mind and intellect gets carried over across incarnations.*
- ❖ *Buddha said that one should be like a well-lit house. If the 'house' is dark, thieves like aggressiveness, arrogance, ego, and a sense of superiority will invade it.*
- ❖ *A deluded mind can never behold and revel in the timeless Brahman.*

11

YOU'RE YOUR FRIEND, YOUR ENEMY TOO

"Bhagavad Gita kinchidathita

Gangajalalavakanika pita

Sakrdapi/yena/murarisamarcha

Kriyate/tasya/yamena/na/charcha

(Bhaja Govindam, bhaja Govindam........)"   (20)

"To one who has studied the Bhagavad Gita even a little, who has sipped at least a drop of water from the Ganga, who has worshipped Lord Murari at least once, there is no discussion (quarrel) with Yama, the Lord of death."

This stanza is believed to have been given out by Sri Anandagiri, another disciple of Adi Sankara.

The study of the Gita, drinking water from the holy river Ganga, and the worship of Lord Murari have been considered sufficient conditions for spiritual evolution. If one can grasp a little bit of the Bhagavad Gita, his/her life will be transformed. The Lord says, "Lift yourself by yourself, do not condemn yourself, for you are your friend and, you are your enemy."

The Gita wisdom makes us understand that by raising our consciousness spiritually and getting established in our indestructible spiritual identity, we can taste real freedom and get rid of all our fears, including the fear of death. In the Gita (4.38), Krishna says, "Verily there exists nothing in the world more noble and sacred than self-knowledge." There is nothing more empowering than transcendental spiritual knowledge.

Ganga stands for spiritual knowledge for the Hindu. It is believed that the river Ganges flows from the head of Lord Shiva and it is considered the river of knowledge. Taking a dip in this river of true knowledge, according to Hinduism, liberates one. It is the eternal river of the knowledge of the Self, flowing from the teacher to the taught in an unbroken perennial stream. To sip a drop of this 'spiritual flow' of Ganga is to enjoy the serenity and fullness of the inner world.

Once we understand our spiritual nature, we get to realize lasting happiness, eternal existence, and knowledge about the Absolute, which are the attributes of our core spiritual identity.

Lord Murari is a 'state of being', a 'state of awakened consciousness.' To worship the Lord is to live and revel in that state of *being* and to live that awakened consciousness. Without annihilating the ego (*Mura*), one cannot hope to attain immaculate peace. This calls for total surrender and devotion at the altar of the very destroyer of ego (*Murari*).

The changes to which the body is subject are the birth, existence, growth, decay, disease, and death. All the pains and sufferings of life are due to these six-fold changes. All the symptoms of mutability experienced by the body are alien to the Self. The Self is Unborn, Eternal, Birthless, and Deathless (*Ajah, Nityah*) (Gita, 2.20). A yogi who has experienced the Self and has transcended and got liberated from the changes the body gets exposed to becomes *Ajah, Nityah* thanks to self-realization. Even the God of death (Yama) will not touch such a person.

Supriya: "But is this verse not oversimplifying the flow of divine blessings, Sir? It says a little bit of reading the Bhagavad Gita, sipping at least a drop of the holy water from Ganga, and worshipping the Lord even for once would remove the fear of death. Is it not giving false hope to most people, who would have done these three things once in a while in life? Can self-realization be that simple?"

Trainer: "We should just not take the superficial meaning of the verse, Supriya. Let me bring clarity to it. The Bhagavad Gita is considered the essence of all the Upanishads. A study of it reveals the hidden essence, the exact goal of human life, and the methods to achieve that goal. A little bit of studying the Gita means understanding the essence and purpose of life through contemplation of the meaning of the Lord's Song.

Similarly, sipping at least a drop of Ganges water means to gain at least a glimpse of the experience of *Brahma vidya* (knowledge about Brahman). The implied suggestion is that one should gain a direct experience of the Brahman and get self-realization, at least equivalent to a drop of the sacred water. As it stands for 'spiritual knowledge', to sip a drop of the holy water means to enjoy the tranquility and fullness of the spiritual being. Swami Chinmayananda writes, "In the context of the stanza, the statement 'who has sipped at least a drop of the Ganga water,' should mean 'those who have at least had a glimpse of the Infinite and the higher possibility of the divine way of living.'

Thirdly, Swami continues, "the body consciousness and the ego-sense, arising out of a false identification with matter, can be rubbed off only by devoted worship and prayer at the altar of the very destroyer of ego (*Murari*)."

So, it is clear that the stanza in question holds a deeper meaning to the terms, like a bit of Gita, a drop of Ganga water, and worship of the Lord at least once than what their apparent meanings suggest. One has to approach these terms and also take to these exercises, namely, studying the Gita, drinking Ganges water, and worshipping the Lord with utmost *shraddha*. Sankara explains *shraddha* as 'that by which an individual readily understands the exact import of the scriptural text as well as the pregnant words of advice of the preceptor." The *sadhak* should be devoted to these divine exercises by giving one's undivided attention to them and by maintaining, in his mind, a continuous consciousness of the Divine. A mere intellectual study of the Gita, a ritualistic sip of the holy water, or a ceremonious prayer 'will not help to purify and shape our 'within' to the glorious Beauty of the Divine.'

The saga of reincarnation

Over to the next verse of *Bhaja Govindam.*

"*Punarapi/jananam/punarapi/maranam*

Punarapi/jananeejattare/sayanam

Iha/samsare/bahudustare

Kripayapare/pahi/murare.

(Bhaja Govindam, bhaja Govindam......)"

(21)

'Again birth, again death, and again lying in mother's womb! This *samsara* process is very difficult to cross over. Save me, Murari (O destroyer of Mura) through the Infinite kindness of Thine.'

This endless cycle of birth and death, and the 'imprisonment' in between in the mother's womb! What is the purpose of this exercise getting repeated again and again? Why must we reincarnate? If we all come from God, then, after death, why don't we simply merge back into Him? These questions were raised once to Paramahamsa Yogananda. He answered thus: "If our individuality gets dissolved by death, we would do so indeed (merge back into God). But **the ego forms the physical body**. It is the cause, not the effect, of physical birth. The ego is an element of the

116

astral body, which is retained after the physical death. The physical body is merely the ego's projection into the material world."

He continued: "God cannot be realized by so simple an act as mere dying. To die is easy, but it is very difficult to attain that high level of consciousness in which the soul can merge back into Infinity. After death, the basic tendencies of a person's nature remain just what they were on earth."

To the question of what causes the ego to reincarnate, Yogananda's response was:

"Desire. Desire, you see, directs energy. As long as a person desires the things of earth, he must come back here, where alone his desires can be fulfilled."

Asked, "Must every desire conceived on earth be fulfilled here only?" the master said: "Not pure desires – not, for example, the longing for beautiful music, expansive scenery, or harmonious relationships. Such desires can be fulfilled better in the astral world than on this imperfect material plane."

(From *The Essence of Self-realization*)

The mystery of reincarnation

'Reincarnation is the religious or philosophical belief that the soul or spirit, after biological death, begins a new life in a new body that may be human, animal, or spiritual depending on the moral quality of the previous life's actions.'

The entire universal process that gives rise to the cycle of death and rebirth, governed by karma, is referred to as *samsara*. Karma (action) may be good or bad. Based on the type of one's karma, a person will be destined to have his subsequent birth. For instance, if one has done a lot of divine service and has a desire to do more such service, after death, his soul will get directed, for rebirth, to a family that is supportive of his unfulfilled desires. According to Hinduism, even Devas may also die and be born again.

In the Bhagavad Gita, Lord Krishna tells Arjuna: "Never was a time when I did not exist, nor you, or all these kings; nor in the future, shall any of us cease to be. As the embodied soul continuously passes, in this body, from childhood to youth to old age, the soul similarly passes into another body at death. A sober person is not bewildered by such a change. Like a person discarding the worn-out garments, worn-out bodies are cast off by the soul indwelling them, and new bodies are donned."

According to Sankara, the world as we understand it is like a dream- fleeting and illusory. To be trapped in *samsara* (the cycle of birth and death) is the result of ignorance of the true nature of our existence. Ignorance (*avidya*) of one's true self leads to ego-consciousness, which grounds one in desire and a perpetual chain of reincarnations. The idea is intricately linked to karma, a concept first recorded in the Upanishads. Every action has a corresponding reaction, and its force determines one's next reincarnation.

(Source: *Indian Journal of Psychiatry, Jan.2013*)

As already stated, desire is the cause of one's rebirth. The mere presence of a body, says Sri Yukteswar, the guru of Yogananda, signifies that its existence is made possible by unfulfilled desires. The stronger the unfulfilled desires on death, the sooner such beings return to earth.

As Swami Chinmayananda writes, "Birth is painful; death.....excruciatingly so and again, to come to life in the horrid cell of the womb, there to be crushed, twisted, imprisoned, and persecuted by the physical and mental strains and jerks of the mother, is indeed abhorrent, terrible, cruel. And yet, as we are today, we are seemingly helpless."

All my karma, my ego, and my burning desires have enslaved me. To free myself from this great inner tyrant, I need now a mighty friend.......who can It be?

"O destroyer of Mura, Lord Krishna, save me........help me, please". This is the ardent prayer unto Him and seeking His feet of love is the only way out."

The only antidote to our ego and the egocentric *vasanas* that propel us to seek carnal pleasures is to surrender unto Him and to sincerely invoke His grace so that divine and godly *vasanas* are created in us. Slowly, our body consciousness will give way to soul consciousness. The Gita declares:

Sarvadharman/parityajya/mamekam/saranam/vraja

Aham/tva/sarvapapebhyo/mokshayisyami ma/suchah

(18.66)

Observes Chinmayananda: "This is the noblest of all the stanzas in the Divine Song, and yet this is the most controversial......To Sri Ramanuja, this is the final verse (*Charama-Shloka*) of the whole *Gita.*" The essence of Swami's interpretation of the stanza is transliterated below.

Every object in the world has two kinds of properties, viz. the essential and the non-essential. Even in the absence of its non-essential qualities, a substance will remain intact if its essential quality stays. This 'essential' property of a substance, like heat in the fire of a flame, irrespective of the size and length of its tongue, is called its *dharma*. The essential *dharma* of man is the 'Divine Spark of Existence,' the Infinite Lord.

The Lord says, *"Sarvadharman / parityajya"* – abandoning all dharma. Why does the Lord ask us to give up all dharma? Due to his identification with the dharmas of the body, mind, and intellect, the finite ego in the seeker is living them (these dharmas) as a mere perceiver, feeler, and thinker. This perceiver-feeler-thinker personality in us is the individuality that expresses itself as the ego. These are but NOT our essential dharmas. And, since these are the non-essentials, renouncing all dharmas means ENDING THE EGO.

To rephrase the above, to renounce here means not to allow ourselves to fall again and again into this state of identification with the outer envelopments of matter around us. It means, renouncing the extrovert tendencies of the mind and developing introspection diligently. This is what is suggested in the phrase 'RENOUNCING ALL DHARMAS.

"Mamekam/saranam/vraja" –come to ME ALONE for shelter. Self-withdrawal from the extrovert nature will be impossible unless the mind is given a positive method of developing its introvert attention. By single-pointed, steady contemplation upon ME (read, the Self), which is the One-without-a-second, we can

accomplish our total withdrawal from the misinterpreting equipment of the body, mind, and intellect.

"Ma shuchah" −be not grieved. During meditation, when the mind gets persuaded away from all its restless occupations with the outer vehicles, and is brought, again and again, to contemplate upon the Self, the Infinite, Lord Krishna wants the seeker to renounce all his ANXIETIES TO REALIZE. Even a desire to realize constitutes a disturbing thought that can obstruct the intended outcome.

"Aham/tva/sarvapapebhyo/mokshayisyami" − I shall release you from all sins. As a seeker renounces more and more of his identifications with his outer envelopments through steady contemplation and meditation upon the Lord of his heart, he grows in his vision. In the newly awakened sensitive consciousness, he becomes more and more poignantly aware of the number of *vasanas* he has to exhaust. In this scenario, the Lord says, "Do not grieve. I shall release you from all sins." Sins here mean the disturbing, desire-breeding, agitation-brewing *vasanas*.

So, Sankara says: *"Bhaja Govindam.........bhaja Govindam......."*

<u>MAJOR TAKEAWAYS</u>

- ❖ *The most noble and sacred knowledge in the world, says the Gita, is self-knowledge.*

- ❖ The Self is Unborn, Eternal, Birthless, and Deathless.

- ❖ The ego forms one's physical body. The ego, being an element of the astral body, is retained even after the physical death.

- ❖ The basic tendencies of a person's nature remain even after the physical death.

- ❖ Unfulfilled desires are the cause of rebirth. The stronger such desires, the sooner the reincarnation.

- ❖ One need not take a rebirth on earth to fulfill pure desires like the longing for beautiful music or harmonious relationships, as these can be achieved much better in the astral world.

❖	Ignorance (avidya) of one's true Self leads to ego-consciousness, which causes desires and consequential reincarnation.

❖	Total surrender to God elevates one from body consciousness to soul consciousness.

❖	Every object has two kinds of properties – the essential and the non-essential. The essential property of a substance/object is called its dharma.

❖	The essential dharma of man is his Divine Spark of Existence.

<u>ACKNOWLEDGMENTS</u>

As Kabir Das, a 15th-century Indian mystic poet and saint, famously said, the Guru first. The spiritual enlightenment, in the most limited and loose sense of the word, I could gain through the long and close association with my Guru, Navajyothisree Karunakaraguru, a Master non-pareil, has facilitated my author-journey through my books immensely. The nuggets of wisdom knocking at the door of my imagination as I was writing the pages of my books were amazing, as these never occurred to me till the moments of truth arrived! That's the power of Guru. I mentally prostrate at thy feet, Master.

I am beholden to the renowned authors and other scholars whose works came in handy for me to gain insights into the different perspectives of the topic of this book.

My thanks are due to my mentor Som Bathla, my colleague Chandralekha (for her support in formatting the book), and to N. Sareej, whose creative mind has brought out beautiful and impressive covers for all my books.

Finally, not because you're the last in the queue, but because, as the consumer of the final product, you appear in the picture only after the above-named, I sincerely thank you, the reader of this book and all the readers and reviewers of my earlier titles. Your encouragements and support have been the fuel in my creative journey. From the bottom of my heart, I thank you for the kind gesture, extended and anticipated (for my future works).

BIBLIOGRAPHY

Chinayananda, Swami (2013). Bhaja Govindam. Chimaya Prakashan, Central Chinmaya Mission Trust, Sandeepany Sadhanalaya, Saki Vihar Road, Powai, Mumbai-400072

Chinmayananda, Swami (2021). The Holy Geeta. Chinmaya Prakashan, Central Chinmaya Mission Trust, Sandeepany Sadhanalaya, Saki Vihar Road, Powai, Mumbai-400072

Deepak Chopra (2008). Power, Freedom and Grace. Hay House Publications (India) Pvt. Ltd. Muskaan Complex, Plot No. 3, B-2 Vasant Kunj, New Delhi 110070

Eckhart Tolle (2002). The Power of NOW. Yogi Impressions Books Pvt. Ltd. 61, Anjali, Minoo Desai Road, Colaba, Mumbai 400005

Jose Silva and Burt Goldman (1988).The Silva Mind Control Method of Mental Dynamics. Palm Springs, California.

Paramahansa Yogananda (1998). Autobiography of a Yogi. Jaico Publishing House, 127 Mahatma Gandhi Road, Fort, Mumbai 400023

Radhakrishnan Pillai (2020) Chanakya Neeti. Jaico Publishing House, A-2 Jash Chambers, 7-A Sir Phirozshah Mehta Road, Fort, Mumbai 400001

Rajagopalachari C (2017). Bhaja Govindam. Bharatiya Vidhya Bhavan, Kulapati K.M.Munshi Marg, Mumbai 400007

Rolf Dobelli (2013). The Art of Thinking Clearly. Hodder & Stoughton Ltd., 338 Euston Road, London NW13 BH

Sukhabodhananda, Swami (2012). Bhaja Govindam: Seeking and Finding Answers Within. Jaico Publishing House, A-2 Jash Chambers, 7-A Sir Phirozshah Mehta Road, Fort, Mumbai 400001

A REQUEST TO THE READER

May I entreat you, my esteemed reader, for a small favor?

First, kindly accept my deep sense of gratitude to you for having bought and read this book. This is the second Volume of the 3-book series based on the epic Poem *Bhaja Govindam*, wherein Sri Sankara has encapsulated the substance of all his *Vedantic works*. I shall be obliged if you could provide me with your valuable rating and a review of the book on the Amazon site. Such a small gesture from your side would be a great support, inspiration, and encouragement for me in my author journey, where I find my passion and mission.

I shall be deeply obliged if you would also get, read, and review my highly rated and much acclaimed other titles, including the 5-book-series named 'Gems of Mahabharata' and the 3-volume series titled 'The Art of Man-Making', many of which have been multiple times international # 1 bestsellers in the U.S.A., the U.K., Australia, and India (a mention of my 13 books is there at the outset of this book).

Thanks, once again.

www.ingramcontent.com/pod-product-compliance
Lightning Source LLC
Chambersburg PA
CBHW020838150726
48196CB00002B/123